Literacy in Action

Authors

Dr. Sharon Jeroski

Andrea Bishop
Jean Bowman
Lynn Bryan
Linda Charko
Maureen Dockendorf
Christine Finochio
Jo Ann Grime
Joanne Leblanc-Haley
Deidre McConnell
Carol Munro
Cathie Peters
Lorraine Prokopchuk
Arnold Toutant

PEARSON

Education
Canada

Grade 6 Project Team

Team Leader and Publisher: Anita Borovilos
National Literacy Consultants: Beth Ecclestone and Norma MacFarlane
Publishers: Susan Green and Elynor Kagan
Product Manager: Donna Neumann
Managing Editor: Monica Schwalbe
Developmental Editors: Chelsea Donaldson, Elaine Gareau, and Mariangela Gentile
Production Editors: Susan Ginsberg, Milena Mazzolin, Adele Reynolds, and Lisa Santilli
Copy Editor: Jessica Westhead
Proofreaders: Rebecca Vogan and Jessica Westhead
Research: Glen Herbert and Rebecca Vogan
Production Coordinators: Donna Brown and Zane Kaneps
Senior Manufacturing Coordinator: Jane Schell
Art Director: Zena Denchik
Designers: Zena Denchik, Maki Ikushima, Anthony Leung, Alex Li, and Word & Image Design
Permissions Research: Cindy Howard
Photo Research: Glen Herbert, Amanda McCormick, and Grace O'Connell
Storyboard Posters: Barbara Boate and Deborah Kekewich
Vice-President Publishing and Marketing: Mark Cobham

ISBN-13: 978-0-13-201736-7 (softcover)
ISBN-10: 0-13-201736-9 (softcover)
ISBN-13: 978-0-13-204739-5 (hardcover)
ISBN-10: 0-13-204739-X (hardcover)

Printed and bound in Canada.
3 4 5 TC 11 10 09

The publisher has taken every care to meet or exceed industry specifications for the manufacture of textbooks. The cover of this sewn book is a premium, polymer-reinforced material designed to provide long life and withstand rugged use. Mylar gloss lamination has been applied for further durability.

PEARSON
Education
Canada

Acknowledgements

Series Consultants

Andrea Bishop
Anne Boyd
Christine Finochio
Don Jones
Joanne Leblanc-Haley
Jill Maar
Joanne Rowlandson
Carole Stickley

Specialist Reviewers

Science: Doug Herridge
  Toronto, ON
Social Studies: Marg Lysecki
  Toronto, ON
Aboriginal: Ken Ealey
  Edmonton, AB

Equity: Dianna Mezzarobba
  Vancouver, BC
Levelling: Susan Pleli
  Stoney Creek, ON
Iris Zammit
  Toronto, ON

Grades 3–6 Advisors and Reviewers

Dr. Frank Serafini
  Assistant Professor,
  University of Las Vegas,
  Las Vegas, Nevada

Patricia Adamson
  Winnipeg, MB
Marion Ahrens
  Richmond Hill, ON
Ray Appel
  Vancouver, BC
Sandra Ball
  Surrey, BC
Gwen Bartnik
  Vancouver, BC
Jennifer Batycky
  Calgary, AB
Michelle Bellavia
  Hamilton, ON
Mary-Jane Black
  Hamilton, ON
Jackie Bradley
  Saskatoon, SK
Diane Campbell
  Durham, ON
Nancy Carl
  Coquitlam, BC
Janet Chow
  Burnaby, BC
Marla Ciccotelli
  London, ON
Susan Clarke
  Burlington, ON
Norma Collinson
  Truro, NS
Lynn Crews
  Lower Sackville, NS
Kathyrn D'Angelo
  Richmond, BC

Pat Dooley
  Nelson, BC
Susan Elliott
  Toronto, ON
Diane Gagley
  Calgary, AB
Michael Gallant
  Calgary, AB
Jennifer Gardner
  Vernon, BC
Adrienne Gear
  Vancouver, BC
Faye Gertz
  Niska, AB
Cindy Gordon
  Victoria, BC
James Gray
  Winnipeg, MB
Kathleen Gregory
  Victoria, BC
Myrtis Guy
  Torbay, NL
Kim Guyette-Carter
  Dartmouth, NS
Jackie Hall
  Vancouver, BC
Natalie Harnum
  Berwick, NS
Sherida Hassanali
  Herring Cove, NS
Deborah Holley
  Duncan, BC
Joanne Holme
  Surrey, BC
Patricia Horstead
  Maple Ridge, BC
Carol Hryniuk-Adamov
  Winnipeg, MB
Pamela Jacob
  Limestone, ON

Joanne Keller
  Delta, BC
Dawn Kesslering
  Regina, SK
Karen Quan King
  Toronto, ON
Linda Kirby
  Sault Ste. Marie, ON
Sheryl Koers
  Duncan, BC
Roger Lacey
  Calgary, AB
Sharon LeClair
  Coquitlam, BC
Catherine Little
  Toronto, ON
Caroline Lutyk
  Burlington, ON
Heather MacKay
  Richmond, BC
Margaret Marion
  Niagara Falls, ON
Sangeeta McAuley
  Toronto, ON
Paula McIntee
  Allanburg, ON
Caroline Mitchell
  Guelph, ON
Laura Mossey
  Durham, ON
Rhonda Nixon
  Edmonton, AB
Gillian Parsons
  Brantford, ON
Linda Perrin
  Saint John, NB
Charolette Player
  Edmonton, AB

Rhonda Rakimov
  Duncan, BC
Tammy Renyard
  Duncan, BC
Kristine Richards
  Windsor, ON
Kathryn Richmond
  St. Catharines, ON
Barbara Rushton
  New Minas, NS
Jaye Sawatsky
  Delta, BC
Michelle Sharratt
  Woodbridge, ON
Cathy Sheridan
  Ottawa, ON
Nanci-Jane Simpson
  Hamilton, ON
Kim Smith
  Newmarket, ON
Candace Spilsbury
  Duncan, BC
Sheila Staats
  Brantford, ON
Patricia Tapp
  Hamilton, ON
Vera Teschow
  Mississauga, ON
Joanne Traczuk
  Sutton West, ON
Sonja Willier
  Edmonton, AB
Susan Wilson
  St. Catharines, ON
Kelly Winney
  London, ON
Beth Zimmerman
  London, ON

CONTENTS

UNIT 1

What Is Fair ? •2

Read Together

No Fair! • 4
> by *Cathie Peters* (cartoons)

Shared

Learn Together Poster

Guided Practice

Fighting for Fairness
> by *Douglas Paton* (biographies)

Kim Kilpatrick: Aiming for Equality • 10

Errol Lee: Rapping for Respect • 12

Zoe Jenkins: Taking Action for Animals • 14

Literacy in Action

Read Biographies 8

Think Like a Reader 9

Reflect on Your Reading 16

Read Like a Writer 17

Independent Practice

Making Waves: Ryan Hreljac's Fight for
Fresh Water • 18
by Diana Federman (biography)

My Grandpa: A Born Fighter • 22
by Sharon Lem (memoir)

Read! Write! Say! Do!

Express Yourself! • 26
(slogans)

Square and Fair • 28
by Clay McLeod (magazine article)

Is It Fair? • 36
(photographs)

At Your Age?! • 38
by Bea Bernstein (play)

Secret of the Dance • 43
by Andrea Spalding and Alfred Scow
(narrative fiction)

Three Monks, No Water • 53
by Ting-xing Ye (modern fable)

Your Literacy Portfolio

Interviewers at Work! 34
Connect and Share 60
Spotlight on Learning 61

UNIT 2

Images for Sale • 62

Read Together

Special Effects   • 64
  adapted by Chelsea Donaldson (explanation)

Shared

Learn Together Poster

Guided Practice

Who's the Audience?
  by Susan Green (advertisements)
Fun Is a Phone Call Away   • 70
Sometimes Good News Can't Wait   • 72
Bringing Families Together   • 74

Literacy in Action

Viewing Images 68
Think Like a Viewer 69
Reflect on Your Viewing 76
View Like a Designer 77

Independent Practice

Giving Credit • 78
  (storyboards/interview)

Cover Up! The Truth Behind Those
Perfect Pictures • 84
  (report/magazine cover)

Read! Write! Say! Do!

What Do You See on TV? • 88
  by Shelagh Wallace
  (information article)

Born to Stand Out! • 96
  by Breanna Myles (poem)

Brand Names vs. Look-Alikes • 98
  (report/survey)

The Other Side • 101
  by Istvan Banyai (images)

A Tangled Web • 107
  by Sara Snow and Susin Nielsen
  (television script)

Your Literacy Portfolio

Producers at Work! 94
Connect and Share 118
Spotlight on Learning 119

The Wonders of Space • 120

Read Together

Space: A Guided Tour • 122
(information article)

Shared

Learn Together Poster

Guided Practice

What's Out There?
by Susan Doyle (explanations)

Space Rocks • 128

Space Junk • 130

Extraterrestrial Life • 132

Literacy in Action

Reading in Science 126
Think Like a Reader 127
Reflect on Your Reading 134
Read Like a Writer 135

Independent Practice

Space Tomatoes! • 136
  by Elizabeth MacLeod (explanation)

A Star Is Born • 140
  by Michael George (explanation)

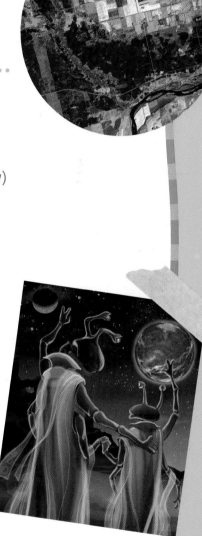

Read! Write! Say! Do!

Canada from Space • 146
  (satellite images)

Pluto No Longer a Planet! • 150
  by Keltie Thomas (fictional news interview)

Ask an Astronaut • 152
  (question and answer)

Coyote Creates the Big Dipper • 157
  by C.J. Taylor (traditional tale)

Secrets • 161
  by Myra Cohn Livingston (poem)

Satellitis • 162
  by Robert Priest (poem)

Captain Arsenio • 164
  by Pablo Bernasconi (narrative fiction)

The Blue Planet • 172
  by Robert J. Sawyer
  (science fiction story)

Your Literacy Portfolio

Researchers at Work! 144
Connect and Share 180
Spotlight on Learning 181

What Is Fair?

LEARNING GOALS

In this unit you will

- Read, listen to, and view biographies about Canadians who have fought for fair treatment.

- Make connections to your life and other situations.

- Discuss images that represent fairness.

- Express your own ideas about fairness in written and oral presentations.

determination
courage
equality
stereotype
point of view
changing values

No Fair!

by Cathie Peters
Illustrated by Dave Whamond

How can families make sure everyone is treated fairly?

"NO FAIR!" It's a familiar cry in most families. Older children complain that their younger siblings get away with more than they should. Little ones see their big brothers and sisters enjoying privileges that they want too. Parents and caregivers struggle to juggle family, work, and personal responsibilities. Sometimes it can seem as if everyone has a complaint!

LET'S TALK ABOUT IT...

- For each situation, identify the problem from each person's perspective. Discuss a solution that would be fair to all.

- With a partner or in a small group, discuss other situations involving family or friends in which fairness is an issue. Choose one of your ideas to dramatize in a scene.

Read Biographies

Authors write biographies about people who have interesting or inspiring lives. A biography tells us about a person's character and achievements.

TALK ABOUT IT!

- Tell a partner or group about a biography you have read or viewed.

- What was interesting about this person?

- What did you learn about this person's character?

Here are some places you can find biographies.

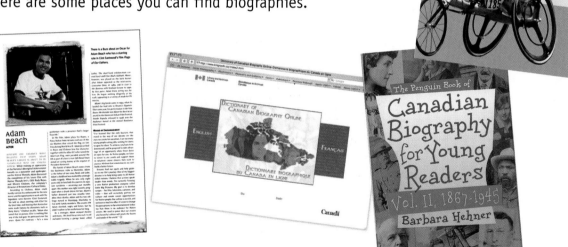

With your partner or group, make a chart like the one below. Fill in the information about people whose biographies you have read or would like to read.

Person	Character traits	Achievements	How he or she made a difference

Think Like a Reader

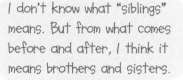
Read with a purpose

■ Why do you read about real people and their lives?

Crack the code

When you come across a word you are unfamiliar with, look at what comes before and after the word. Then think about what makes sense.

Make meaning

Practise using these strategies when you read biographies:

PREDICT Look at the title, headings, and pictures for clues. What do you predict this selection will be about?

PAUSE AND CHECK As you read, think about your predictions. Were you right? Make new predictions about the rest of the text.

CONNECT Think about how the biography relates to your own life or the lives of others you know about.

Analyze what you read

■ Biographies often tell events from the author's point of view. Why is it important to consider the point of view of other people who know or knew the person?

Kim Kilpatrick
Aiming for Equality

Brief Bio

- Won several Paralympic medals in swimming

- Became first blind camp counsellor at the YMCA

- Founded a camp for blind children

PREDICT

What kind of equality is Kim aiming for?

If you were drowning and someone saved you, would you care if that person was blind? Of course you wouldn't! Kim Kilpatrick feels the same way.

Kim has been blind since birth, but she has never let her blindness get in the way of her goals. By age 14, she had become an expert swimmer. In fact, she won two silver medals and one gold medal at the 1980 Paralympics.

Leader in Training

At age 15, Kim wanted to be a camp counsellor at a local YMCA camp. The camp had never had a blind counsellor before. Camp organizers weren't sure Kim would be able to handle the job. She met with the organizers to plead her case and convinced them to let her try their Leaders in Training program.

That summer, Kim passed the first level. She managed canoe trips and camping. She also worked in various areas of the camp. Then she had to earn her Bronze Medallion, the certificate that all lifeguards must have. She attended all the lessons, but the instructor would not let her take the final test. He did not think a blind person would be able to work as a lifeguard.

The next year, Kim appealed the decision and won her case. And, of course, she also passed the test! At the end of the summer, Kim had qualified to work as a camp counsellor. At age 16, she was the first blind person to hold this position.

Helping Others

By the time Kim was in university, she was well aware that many blind children had few chances to get together to join in activities. So she started a camp for blind children in the Ottawa area. "I started the camp once a week for a few weeks as a volunteer," she said. "It expanded, and I was hired for the next couple of summers to be one of the coordinators." That camp is still in operation today.

Kim currently works for Volunteer Ottawa. She helps people with disabilities find volunteer work in the Ottawa area. She also works as a storyteller and music therapist.

PAUSE AND CHECK

What do you think Kim will do next?

CONNECT

What other people or situations does Kim's story remind you of?

The Paralympics is a sports event in which people with physical challenges can demonstrate their achievements.

"Like others with physical challenges, I had to find ways to adapt to things, but I also learned to speak up when something wasn't working."

11

Errol Lee
Rapping for Respect

Brief Bio

- Immigrated to Canada from Jamaica in 1977

- Organized an anti-drug concert at age 17

- Released successful CDs in 2001 and 2004

PREDICT

How can a musician work for fairness?

For some people, it would be hard to put aside a promising career as a musician to talk to young people about fairness. For Errol Lee, the decision was easy.

Errol was born in Kingston, Jamaica, in 1968. His family was very poor, but music was always an important part of their lives. Errol's father was a music producer and his mother was a singer.

Errol's mother wanted to give him a better life, so she brought him to Canada. He was eight years old. By the time Errol was 15, he was already working on his first recordings. He was starting his music career, but he was also getting into trouble. During his early teens, Errol struggled to find his way.

A Change of Heart

During the tough times, it was Errol's grandmother who helped him the most. She had always taught him to believe in himself and to care for others. He began to realize that he was not treating himself, or others, fairly.

At age 17, Errol was on the way to musical success. He then decided to make a change. He refocused his music and its message to help other young people. He wanted kids to learn that no matter how unfair life might seem, it's what you think and how you act that define who you are. He also wanted to encourage empathy, the ability to feel what another person is feeling. "Empathy," he says, "helps you to be fair. It puts you in other people's shoes so you can understand what they are feeling."

Cool to Be Kind

Errol now tours schools around the world performing for kids. He uses a high-energy combination of music, dancing, and speaking to get kids involved in helping others. One of his main messages is: "It's cool to be kind. It's uncool to be cruel."

PAUSE AND CHECK

What do you think Errol will do next?

CONNECT

What other people or situations does Errol's story remind you of?

Let's Put the Brakes on Bullying!

"Character matters. It's not enough to be positive in life. You have to be positive toward others."

Zoe Jenkins
Taking Action for Animals

Brief Bio

- Born on January 9, 1993

- Formed EARTH, an animal rights group

- Organized a demonstration, in 2005, to help marine animals

PREDICT

What can a young person do to fight for fairness?

Can kids really do anything to fight for fairness? Thirteen-year-old Zoe Jenkins feels they can. Zoe is the founder of an animal rights group called EARTH (Every Animal's Right to Hope). Along with other members of EARTH, Zoe is working to "ensure the fair treatment of every animal, ensure the conservation of wildlife worldwide, and raise empathy and respect for animals...."

EARTH Is Born

Zoe was inspired by Craig Kielburger, the young founder of Free the Children. In 2004, she and her friends saw a film at school about him. Craig started a children's rights organization when he was only 12 years old. When Zoe heard about him, she realized that even young people can achieve a lot if they are willing to work for what they believe in. This inspiration gave her the idea to start EARTH.

Protests and Plans

The group's first activity was a fundraiser for the Humane Society in December 2004. It was a big success. EARTH soon decided to work on something even bigger. Zoe and the other members wanted to improve the situation for the sea creatures in marine zoos.

Zoe did some research on marine zoos. She concluded that tanks were too small and the animals' diets were not healthy. She also felt the animals spent too much time around humans. This contact meant they could never be released.

In January 2005, EARTH helped organize a demonstration outside a marine zoo. "Eventually," said Zoe, "we would like to see the zoo stop keeping whales. Right now, though, we're trying to get better enclosures."

Zoe knows that change takes time and persistence. She and the other EARTH members plan to keep working toward their goals—just as Craig Kielburger did.

PAUSE AND CHECK

What do you think Zoe will do next?

CONNECT

What other people or situations does Zoe's story remind you of?

Animal rights activists feel that it is cruel to keep large animals such as whales in small tanks.

"If you're not willing to go far to help animals, then you're really not going to get anything done, because you'll be told that things won't be changed and you'll give up."

15

Reflect on Your Reading

You have . . .

- talked about fairness.
- read biographies about people who fight for fairness.
- explored words and phrases related to these people and the issues they fight for.

respect

equality

empathy

activist

character   persistence

Fairness to me means everyone gets the same opportunities. What do you think?

PREDICT

PAUSE AND CHECK

CONNECT

You have also . . .

- explored different reading strategies.

Write About Learning

When you use the "connect" strategy, you link the new information you are reading to what you already know. Write about how making these connections can help you to understand and enjoy biographies, as well as other forms of writing.

Read Like a Writer

The selections in "Fighting for Fairness" are *biographies*.
Biographies contain important information about a person's life.

TALK ABOUT IT!

- How does the writer get you interested in the topic?

- What kinds of events from the people's lives are included? What events are left out?

- How does the writer use quotations?

Make a chart to show what you know about how biographies are organized.

HINT!

Look at how the writing is **organized**.

How Biographies Are Organized
- begin with an interesting event or hint about what is to come
- tell important events in order
- use time words such as "at first," "later," "that summer," and "in January 2002"

Making Waves:

Ryan Hreljac's Fight for Fresh Water

by Diana Federman

READ LIKE A WRITER

What words and phrases help you to keep track of when events took place?

I magine that you have to fetch and carry every drop of water that you use. Three times a day, you walk for many kilometres to a well and carry home water weighing 20 kilograms. You don't go to school because your water-carrying takes up so much time. On top of all this, the water in the well is not treated. It often makes you sick, but it is the only water you have, so you drink it. Is that fair?

Ryan Hreljac (HURL-jack) doesn't think so, and he has dedicated his time to changing the situation, one well at a time. This young Canadian is what you might call a water ambassador.

Ryan travels the world to tell people how they can help solve a big problem: the lack of safe drinking water in many developing countries. "Everybody can do something," Ryan says.

How can a student from Canada help a village in Africa?

In many developing countries, people carry water for several kilometres from wells to their homes.

Ryan's efforts did not begin in a far-off place, though. They began right at home, in Kemptville, Ontario. In 1998, when he was six years old, Ryan learned from his teacher that children in Africa must often walk for kilometres each day to find water.

Ryan decided to act. He did chores for his parents and neighbours, to raise money. Later, he spoke at schools, churches, and clubs about his goal to collect enough money to build a well in Africa. The word spread, and donations began coming in. After several months of hard work, Ryan had raised $2000, enough to dig one well.

The First Well

An organization called Canadian Physicians for Aid and Relief (CPAR) chose a site for the well in the village of Agweo, Uganda, in central east Africa. Agweo's closest water supply was a swampy area about five kilometres away. The water in the swamp carried several diseases, including typhoid. About one in every five children born in the region died before the age of five. A well in the village would provide cleaner water and would save villagers from making the long trip every day to fetch water.

AFRICA

UGANDA

Ryan and his pen pal, Jimmy, when they were younger

Ryan began writing to a pen pal in Agweo, Jimmy Akana. Jimmy was nine years old, and his parents had disappeared in a civil war. In 2000, CPAR arranged for Ryan and his family to visit Uganda for the opening ceremony of the well. On this trip, Ryan met Jimmy for the first time, and they formed a close friendship—a friendship that would later save Jimmy's life.

The Ripple Effect

After the first well, "the ripple effect took over," Ryan says, "and one goal led to another." With adult help, Ryan founded the Ryan's Well Foundation in 2003 to help people learn about the vital importance of water.

That same year, things began to change in Jimmy Akana's life, as well. The war in Uganda put his life in danger. He needed to get out of Uganda quickly, so Ryan's parents got permission for Jimmy to come to Canada. The Hreljac household has been Jimmy's home ever since.

In the years that followed, Ryan and Jimmy grew up, and the foundation grew along with them. By 2007, it had raised more than $1.5 million and had built 255 wells. Thanks to Ryan, more than 400 000 people in 12 countries now have access to clean water.

Ryan has received countless awards for his work. In 2003, he was presented with the Order of Ontario, the province's highest honour. "The only reason I accept awards," he says, "is that each word I say when I get one might help one more person."

A Typical Kid

These days, Ryan is a busy student who plays football and ice hockey. He also likes studying computer technology. Ryan says he doesn't know what career he will choose. He thinks he may be a lawyer or teacher, or maybe even prime minister! Ryan travels less during the school year now than when he was younger. He explains that his teachers "are a lot stricter now about missing classes."

Ryan has been asked if he ever feels discouraged by the fact that many people still lack good water. He says, "It's important to be an optimist. When people are dying on the other side of the world, to sit in your house and say, 'I can't really help,' that's not the person I want to be. I'm just a typical kid. I had a small dream, and I stayed with it. Everybody can do something."

In 2006, Ryan (right) was invited to speak at the Western Academy of Beijing's International Day.

DIG DEEPER

1. Ryan Hreljac has achieved a great deal in a short time. Create an illustrated timeline showing the main events in Ryan's life so far.

2. Write a letter to Ryan explaining what you admire most about what he did and why you think his actions have inspired so many people.

My Grandpa
A Born Fighter
Shack Jang Mack (1909–2003)

by Sharon Lem

READ LIKE A WRITER

How do the headings help to highlight the main events?

Shack Jang Mack was born on September 9, 1909 in Canada. In this photograph, he is with his granddaughter, Sharon Lem.

How can we correct the wrongs of the past?

Some of my favourite memories are of my grandfather. Grandpa Mack loved to make me laugh. I break into a smile every time I think of his visits when he would take my brothers and me to the CNE (Canadian National Exhibition). Afterward, we would whip up an enormous chocolate cake and devour the whole thing.

As I got older, I realized Grandpa had a wealth of life experiences that I only appreciated with time. Since his passing on March 15, 2003, at age 94, I've been grieving, but at the same time I'm very proud to call him my grandpa. He was very much like everyone else's grandpa, except for one thing—he's a symbol of the unfair treatment the Chinese in Canada suffered at the turn of the century.

Coming to Canada

The story of Grandpa Mack is the story of many Canadian immigrants. Grandpa's father, Mack Cheung Fun, came to Canada in 1865 to pave the way for Grandpa and his three brothers. They all had to pay a special tax called a head tax. Only Chinese immigrants had to pay the tax, which was equal to about two years' salary back then. The government hoped the tax would discourage Chinese people from coming to Canada.

Grandpa grew up in Canada, went to school, learned English, and trained as a chef. After working a few more years, he saved enough money to open his first restaurant. Around this time, his mother urged him to return to China to get married. Grandpa finally gave in and went back in 1928.

Building Canada's Railway

Between 1881 and 1885, thousands of Chinese labourers were brought to Canada to help build the first railway across the country. Many of the workers died doing the dangerous work. Once the railway was complete, the government made it very difficult for Chinese people to stay in Canada or bring their families over.

A head tax identification card

MEDIA WATCH

Watch three different local television news shows. Which groups are represented as reporters or in other on-air roles? How well do the news shows represent Canada's diversity?

He was betrothed to my grandmother, Gat Nuy Ng Shee. But Grandpa was unable to bring Grandma back here with him. That's because in 1923, the government passed the Exclusion Act. The Act barred any Chinese people from immigrating to Canada.

Grandma gave birth to their first child, a boy. By this time, Grandpa was in Canada. The son died before Grandpa had a chance to hold him.

Back and Forth

During Grandpa's years living alone in Canada, he opened a string of restaurants across Manitoba—in The Pas, Sherrigordon, Cold Lake, and Churchill—before settling in Tisdale, Saskatchewan. In the kitchen, Grandpa would cook steaks, burgers, fries, and French toast. Gradually, he would introduce more exotic menu items like chow mein. He became best known for his awesome cheesecake.

Every time he left Canada to go back to China to raise his children, he would sell his café. Upon his return he'd open up another one. This happened five times over four decades. The names of the cafés would change. The first was the M.C. Café, which became the Elite Café, then the Paris Café, and the Roxy Café. My mother, Sue Lynn, was born during the Elite Café period. Then came Uncle Ted, Uncle Yow, Aunt May, and Uncle Willie.

Fighting for Fairness

During his later years, my grandpa took up the fight against the head tax issue, with the help of the Chinese Canadian National Council. They asked for an apology and a payment from the federal government. It is a small amount, but Grandpa thought the payment was important.

"It means the government of Canada thinks I am an equal. That I am not a second-class citizen. That the government is willing to right a wrong," he said.

But even before he began the fight, Grandpa remained a little doubtful. "I don't think I'll get the head tax back from the federal government before I die, and I'm one of the last of my kind."

He was right.

The Government of Canada Apologizes

On June 22, 2006, the federal government apologized for the head tax and for banning Chinese immigrants with the Exclusion Act. The government also offered the few remaining survivors and their spouses a symbolic payment.

DIG DEEPER

Event	How he felt

1. Work with a partner to make a two-column chart showing the major events in Shack Jang Mack's life. In the second column, write words and phrases that tell how he might have felt about each event.

2. Write a biography of someone you know who fought for fairness. Describe the situation this person faced. How did he or she feel about it? What did he or she do? Use headings to highlight the main events.

EXPRESS Yourself!

How can slogans encourage people to think about fairness?

SAVE THE EARTH
It's the only planet with
CHOCOLATE

what if
they gave a war
and everyone
brought
crayons

WANT LESS

I'm not a nugget

IF YOU'RE NOT OUTRAGED, YOU'RE NOT PAYING ATTENTION

I WILL NOT ADVERTISE YOUR COMPANY ON MY T SHIRT

DIG DEEPER

1. With a partner, choose three slogans that appeal to you. Be ready to explain, in your own words, what each one is trying to express.

2. Choose an issue that is important to you. Create your own button, T-shirt, or poster about the issue. Share your design in a group.

Square and FAIR

by Clay McLeod

28

The Bitter Truth About Chocolate

It's the world's favourite sweet treat. We eat three million tonnes of it every year. But most farmers who grow the cocoa beans to make our beloved chocolate are desperately poor.

Many, many people around the world grow cocoa, so farmers cannot demand a fair price for their crop. Big companies that buy cocoa can shop around until they find farmers who will sell their crop cheaply.

Because cocoa is cheap, wages for people who work on the farms are very low. Many families are so poor, children are forced to work on cocoa farms and can't go to school. United Nations reports say that more than a quarter of a million kids are working in dangerous conditions on cocoa farms in West Africa. They harvest cocoa beans with big knives. Without protective gear such as masks, they spray crops with poisonous pesticides. Most kids who work on cocoa farms have never even tasted chocolate.

Seventy percent of the world's chocolate comes from the west coast of Africa. Canada buys millions of cocoa products from that area each year. For this reason, Save the Children Canada and other organizations are encouraging Canadians to buy chocolate that is guaranteed to be farmed without child labour. This kind of chocolate has the fair trade certified logo on its wrapper.

READ LIKE A WRITER

Find three examples in which the author shows how one action causes another.

A 14-year-old boy clears a cocoa field in Côte d'Ivoire. Up to 15 000 children from some of the poorest countries in West Africa are working on cocoa plantations.

From BEAN to BAR

Nothing better than a bite of your favourite chocolate bar? The delicious cocoa you love travels great distances to tickle your taste buds.

Equator

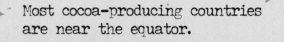

Most cocoa-producing countries are near the equator.

1

Cocoa comes from the tropical cacao (ka-kow) tree. Most cacao trees grow in West Africa, South America, and Asia.

2

When it's time to harvest the cocoa, the farmers cut cacao pods off the trees with machetes.

3

Then farmers break the pods and scoop out the cocoa beans.

Once the beans ferment and dry in the sun, the farmers sell the beans to a local buyer or fair trade co-op. Beans are shipped to factories, usually in Europe. **4**

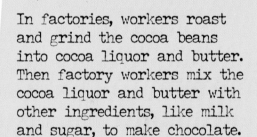

5

In factories, workers roast and grind the cocoa beans into cocoa liquor and butter. Then factory workers mix the cocoa liquor and butter with other ingredients, like milk and sugar, to make chocolate.

Then businesses package the chocolate and distribute it to stores where you can buy it. **6**

Making Trade FAIR

The fair trade logo. When a big company sells 100 chocolate bars, about $6 goes to farmers. When a fair trade company sells 100 bars, about $35 goes to farmers.

Fair trade is a growing movement involving close to a million farmers around the world. Supporters believe that farmers in poor countries should get a fair price for crops such as cocoa beans, coffee, tea, sugar, and bananas so they can support themselves and their families. Fair trade also makes sure craftspeople get a fair deal on the clothing and household items they sell.

Fair trade companies guarantee cocoa farmers a fair price for their beans—sometimes twice what many big companies pay. Fair trade companies also guarantee that farmers will have buyers for years to come. This guarantee helps farmers save—and borrow—money to buy food, clothes, and medicines, and to pay school fees so kids can go to school.

Chocolate with cocoa or other ingredients that were farmed by child labourers can't be fair trade certified. Kids can help on their family's farm, but they must go to school and must not do dangerous work. In Canada, the fair trade logo also means that the cocoa beans were produced without harming the environment. Fair trade chocolate sometimes costs more, but fans are happy to spend their money supporting cocoa farmers and their families.

A school supported by fair trade

Where Do Your Chocolate Dollars <u>GO</u>?

Chew on this! It's not just big chocolate companies and cocoa farmers who profit from chocolate sales. "Coyotes" (as they're called in the Dominican Republic) are people who make money by buying cheap cocoa beans and reselling them at a higher price. When a fair trade company buys a farmer's beans, the beans are sold directly to an international fair trade chocolate manufacturer. So profits from the sale of the beans go to the farmer and back to the community—instead of into coyotes' pockets.

A labourer spreads cocoa beans out to dry in the sun.

A SWEET Way to Make a Difference

1. Spread the word about fair trade chocolate:
- Write a letter to the editor of your local newspaper and encourage people to buy fair trade chocolate.
- Write a postcard to your local grocery store asking it to sell fair trade chocolate.

2. Suggest that your school chooses fair trade chocolate for its next fundraiser.

3. Learn more about fair trade.

DIG DEEPER

1. How has fair trade changed the lives of farmers and their families? Create a web to illustrate your answer.

2. Work with a partner. Write a short radio commercial that persuades shoppers to buy fair trade chocolate, coffee, or crafts. Present your commerical to the class.

Interviewers at Work!

An interview is one way to learn about someone's life. During an interview on a television talk show, the host asks questions about the guest's accomplishments. Sometimes other guests also tell what they know about the person.

Now it's your turn to role-play an interview.

Research Your Subject

- With a partner, choose someone you would like to interview. It might be a real person who has fought for fairness. It might be a character who made a difference in a novel or a movie.

- Make notes from your research or rereading. What was the issue? What action did the person take? What was the result?

- What information about the person's life would you need to tell his or her story?

Plan Your Interview

- Write an introduction that explains how this person fought for fairness.

- Think of interesting questions that will let the audience know important information about the person.

- Prepare answers that tell the audience how the subject felt or what motivated him or her.

PRESENTING TIPS

- Think of a talk show on television that might interview your subject.

- Watch to see how the host introduces the guests.

Present Your Interview

- Decide who will be the interviewer and who will role-play the subject.

- Include props or costumes.

- Present your talk-show interview to the class.

- Invite class members to ask other questions.

- Afterward, think about what went well and where you could have improved your performance. Use feedback from the audience to help you reflect.

When and where were you born?

What has been your greatest challenge?

What are your major accomplishments?

Who has influenced you?

35

What can images say about the issue of fairness?

Is It Fair?

DIG DEEPER

1. Work with a partner. Describe how each of these images represents an issue related to fairness. Then think of a caption for each image.

2. Collect other images that raise the issue of fairness. Choose one image to present to the class.

At YOUR Age?!

by Bea Bernstein

Illustrated by Anne Villeneuve

What might a young person and an older person have in common?

The sound of a motorcycle is heard from offstage.

MAN: *(from offstage)* HEY! WATCH IT, GRANDMA!

BEA: *(enters wearing a leather jacket and carrying a helmet)* Watch where you're walkin'! *(to audience)* Grandma?! I should be so lucky. They see white hair on a motorcycle, suddenly I have grandchildren?

MALCOLM: *(enters wearing a leather jacket)* Hey, Grandma! How about giving me a ride on your bike?

BEA: Get away from me, kid.

MALCOLM: Don't call me "kid."

BEA: Don't call me "Grandma."

MALCOLM: Sorry, I thought all old ladies liked to be called "Grandma."

BEA: Not this one. "Old lady" is not so hot, either. My name's Bea.

MALCOLM: Nice to meet you, Bea. I'm Malcolm. *(they shake hands)* I've never seen an old...er, a grand...um. Way to ride that bike!

BEA: Thanks, Malcolm. Years of practice.

MALCOLM: Why don't you like being called "Grandma"?

BEA: 'Cuz I don't have grandchildren, for one. And 'cuz people usually call me that when they're trying to say I'm too old for something.

MALCOLM: That's *exactly* how I feel about people calling me "kid." They say "kid," but what they mean is...well...I'm too young to think for myself.

BEA: And people think I'm too old to think for myself.

MALCOLM: They think you don't matter as much 'cuz of your age?

BEA: Exactly. No respect.

(Pause.)

MALCOLM: I like your jacket.

BEA: I like yours, too. Wanna know a secret?

MALCOLM: Always!

BEA: My daughter *hates* it when I wear this jacket. She thinks I'm trying to pretend I'm a teenager. She'd rather I wore frilly dresses and hats? Feh! Let me tell ya—hats and motorcycles don't mix.

MALCOLM: I know! My mom feels the same way about my jacket! She thinks I'm trying to look like a teenager. She says this jacket is gonna make me grow up too fast.

BEA: You know, come to think of it, we have a lot in common.

MALCOLM: Yeah. *(pause)* But, y'know what reeeeeally makes me angry!?

BEA: What?

MALCOLM: Getting laughed at for liking things I'm not supposed to like "at my age."

BEA: You're tellin' me!

MALCOLM: Yeah! Like, for instance, I like to play shuffleboard and...I like to rock.

BEA: That's not so unusual! *(demonstrates a dance move)* Everybody likes to rock!

MALCOLM: In a rocking chair?

BEA: *(guffaws)* Come again?

MALCOLM: *(a little hurt)* I like to rock in a rocking chair. I find it soothing.

BEA: Oh. Well, better you than me. Y'know what I find soothing?

MALCOLM: What?

BEA: *(whispers)* My game system.

MALCOLM: *(bursts out)* YOU'VE GOT A GAME SYSTEM?

BEA: Not so loud! Everyone will want to play.

MALCOLM: I've never understood those things.

BEA: It takes practice.

MALCOLM: Would you show me how?

BEA: I guess I could. But I get to go first!

MALCOLM: Cool.

(They start to exit.)

MEDIA WATCH

Look in the newspaper. How are older people portrayed in pictures and words? How are younger people portrayed? Is there any evidence of stereotyping? Explain.

41

BEA: So, you like shuffleboard? Is it hard?

MALCOLM: It's easy...I'll show ya!

BEA: Promise you won't laugh?

MALCOLM: As long as you promise not to laugh at me when I lose on the game system.

BEA: Deal.

(BEA and MALCOLM exchange high fives and exit.)

DIG DEEPER ·····················

1. A stereotype is a fixed image of a certain group of people that ignores their individual differences. In what ways are Bea and Malcolm the victims of stereotypes? Discuss in a group.

2. Write a scene in which Malcolm introduces Bea to his family (or vice versa). What might the family say and how might Malcolm and Bea react?

Secret of the Dance

by Andrea Spalding and Alfred Scow
Illustrated by Darlene Gait

Watl'Kina   1935

Can there be different perspectives on what is fair?

In 1885, the Canadian government passed a law forbidding Aboriginal peoples from holding ceremonies, including the Potlatch. The government official in charge of these efforts was known as the Indian Agent. Potlatches were held by many West Coast First Nations for special occasions, such as marriage, naming children, and mourning the dead. They involved performances of dances owned by the host, who distributed gifts to all the guests. Ceremonies such as the Potlatch were at the heart of these Aboriginal cultures, and so they were continued in secrecy.

This story is based on a true incident in the life of Watl'kina (WALS-kee-nay). Today, Watl'kina is also known as retired judge Alfred Scow, an Elder of the Kwakwa'ka'wakw (KWAK-kwa-kew-wak) Nations. When he was a child, Alfred and his family faced unfairness head on. This is their story.

READ LIKE A WRITER

Why have some parts of the text been set apart?

Many years ago, when the world and I were younger, my family defied the government.

"Dancing's against the law," announced the Indian Agent.

"We need to hold a Potlatch ceremony," whispered the Elders. We were sent out to play.

"The salmon are running," explained the Elders. "We should follow." We helped pack the boat with food and clothing, everything needed for a fishing trip. "Sleep," said Mother. "Dawn will come early."

The baby and my sisters slept. I was too excited. That night, I heard noises outside. I peeked as strangely shaped, blanket-wrapped parcels were hidden in the boat.

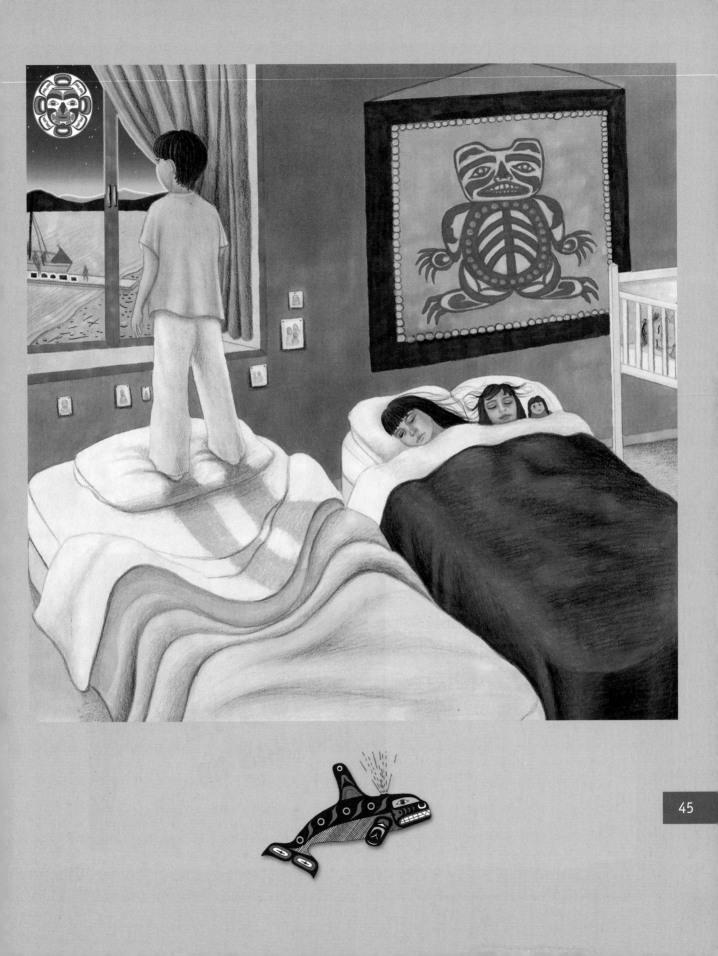

"Watl'kina, help your grandmother into the boat," called Father.

"Careful, Ga'Gaas (GA-gus)," I said as I steadied her arm.

The fish boat sailed through the dawn light. Beyond the islands, the wind was fresh and the waves danced. Dolphins leapt, Eagles soared, and passing Orcas spouted.

"See, we have their blessing," said Ga'Gaas. Father scanned the ocean. No government boats were following.

After World War I, the government made efforts to stop the ceremonies by raiding Potlatches. Once caught, people were given a choice between going to prison and having their masks and other ceremonial regalia taken away.

In 1935, Alfred's family sailed from Gilford Island to the village of Kingcome at the head of the Kingcome Inlet. There, a branch of the family hosted a forbidden Potlatch as a memorial for Alfred's grandfather. Alfred and his sisters were told they couldn't attend. If the Potlatch had been raided, any children found there would have been removed from their parents' care.

It was almost evening when we came to the village huddling between forest and the shore. We anchored in the river. Our relatives fetched us in a canoe.

Mother took me to one side. "We need your help, Watl'kina. Father and I must join the Elders. The children should not come in case the Indian Agent followed us. There may be trouble." I nodded. Mother drew the curtains and tucked us into bed. My throat ached with disappointment.

We watched through the gap in the curtains. Shadowy figures carried the blanket parcels from the boats to the Gookji (GUKE-jee), the Big House. We listened, but heard only a low murmur of voices, the wind in the cedars, and the waves on the shore. Finally, my sisters slept. I crept to the window and lifted the curtain.

The village was dark. Even the dogs were silent. But the drums made the air vibrate. The singing grew louder. It was more than I could stand. I crept out into the night.

"Aiii, Aiii hooooo," chanted voices.

DAA, ta ta ta. DAA, ta ta ta, called the drums.

My feet tapped in response, and I followed the sound, dancing along down the village street.

Suddenly I heard rustlings and movement. Strange masked figures surrounded me. Ga'Gaas' stories had come to life. Eagle, Whale, Raven, Bear, Wolf, even Dzunukwa (DZOO-no-quaa), the Wild Woman, towered over me.

I turned to run.

The Wild Woman grasped my shoulder. My knees trembled. "It is good you see us," murmured Dzunukwa, "for this may be the last time we dance. Watch for the Hamatsa."

The drums called again, and the doors were flung open. The figures left me to enter the Big House. I darted between the closing doors and hid in the shadows. Fire was the only light. It glinted on the button blankets and masks as the dancers circled, weaving in and out of the smoke.

I saw Bear, my clan symbol. He passed right by me. I could not mistake his sharp claws and fierce white teeth. In the firelight he was a real bear, called onto the floor to dance his story.

The Hamatsa appeared from behind the screen. He danced in and out of the shadows. There was something familiar about him. Something in the way he moved and proudly held his head.

I stared, but the flames flickered. I could not see his face. The Hamatsa danced beyond the fire. A log cracked and flared. For a brief moment the shadows were banished.

I knew him.

That was the only time I ever saw my father dance.

Before the dancers finished, I sneaked back to bed. My parents and I never spoke of that night. The masks were re-wrapped in blankets and hidden from the authorities for many years.

Now I am older than my father was when he danced. Each time I step in procession and wear the regalia forbidden him, I rejoice. Tears cloud my eyes as I watch the dancers. For now the government invites us to dance, to honour visiting kings and queens and other guests.

Life makes strange circles. Hehmaas. That is everything.

Many of Alert Bay's masks were confiscated in 1921 and only returned to the people of the Kwakwa'ka'wakw Nations in 1979. They are now on public display in Alert Bay's U'mista Centre. They watch from the walls as the traditional dances are taught to today's children.

In 1951, the government recognized that the law was unfair, and it was repealed.

DIG DEEPER

1. What do you think the author means by "life makes strange circles"? Write a short journal entry describing your interpretation.

2. What are two questions you still have about the banning of the Potlatch? Research the answers to share with the class.

THREE MONKS, NO WATER

by Ting-xing Ye   Illustrated by Harvey Chan

What happens when no one wants to take responsibility?

Once upon a time, there was a mountain; on that mountain, there stood a temple; and in that temple, all alone, lived a young monk.

Besides sweeping the temple, dusting the Buddha statues, and replacing the burned incense sticks every day, the young monk would pray, meditate, and recite the scripture while beating rhythmically on a wooden block. It was a simple and peaceful life as he followed his vows in the service of Buddhism.

There was no water up in the temple, but there was a clear, cold stream at the foot of the mountain. Each morning, the young monk had to make his way down a narrow, winding trail to fetch water, carrying a shoulder pole with a wooden bucket dangling from each end. On the way down the mountain, the empty buckets danced left and right, right and left, in rhythm with his steps. But on the way back, the pole was bowed by the heavy buckets, and it dug painfully into his shoulders.

Rain or shine, hot or cold, dry or damp, the young monk never missed a day lugging his burden up to the temple. With two buckets of water for drinking, cooking, and washing, he even had enough left over to start a vegetable garden. But how he wished someone else could help him someday!

One day the temple had a visitor. He was a middle-aged, tall, and skinny monk, and his robe was sweaty and dusty from travelling. The young monk offered his tired guest fresh spring water and carefully cooked vegetables from the garden. After the meal, the young monk invited the skinny monk to stay in the temple and be company for him. His new companion accepted gracefully.

READ LIKE A WRITER
What interesting details does the writer use to help you visualize what is happening?

The next morning, when it was time to fetch water, they agreed that both of them should go down the mountain together. "That's only fair," they thought to themselves, "since we both will use the water."

But they soon discovered that the carrying-pole was too short to have two buckets placed in the middle while one of them shouldered each end, so they left one bucket behind. Nevertheless, on the way back to the temple they had to stop twice to adjust the bucket. It didn't matter whether the skinny monk was at the front or the back, the bucket would always slide down to the young monk's end and bang painfully against his legs.

With almost half of the water having slopped over the rim of the bucket, they finally struggled into the temple. That day they had barely enough water for drinking and cooking, and none for washing.

Instead of meditating that evening, they were both thinking the same thing: "Maybe tomorrow we will have enough water for the vegetable garden."

Long rainless days descended on the mountain; everything grew as dry as a bone. The two monks peered into the hot blue sky, licking their parched lips, wondering where the clouds had gone. In the garden the beans became scrawny and wrinkled. The green leaves of the cabbages turned yellow, and the tomato plants shrank into dry vines, hanging down helplessly along the wood sticks. With one bucket of water a day, the monks had only a few drops left for the vegetables when the day ended.

While passing the half-empty bucket on the way to their afternoon meditation, each threw an angry glance at the other. But not one word was said.

One afternoon, the temple had another visitor, a big fat monk, carrying a case full of books. When he was offered a drink, he helped himself to two full bowls. After the meal, he asked his two new friends if he could be of help in the temple and be company for them. The young and the skinny monks stared at each other for a moment, then silently nodded their heads.

While they were beating wooden blocks and chanting scriptures that night, all three of them were thinking to themselves.

"I don't need to carry water any more," the young monk thought with full certainty. "I am younger than both of them, not to mention the fact that they are newcomers. They'd better not forget that taking care of a youngster is one of their commitments. Now, finally, my wish comes true." He almost burst into a smile.

"I bet my water-fetching days are over," the skinny monk thought confidently, with a grin on his face. "Clearly I am not as strong as they are because I am the eldest. Besides, since both of them are almost the same height, no one has to grab the bucket to keep it from sliding along the pole."

"Why should I break their daily routine?" the fat monk assured himself. "They know the path and are very skilled in carrying water. But most importantly, I am a scholar and full of knowledge. Everyone knows a scholar is not expected to do any physical labour." He confirmed his thought with a firm nod.

The next day, the sun rose and set, but the buckets remained empty. They shared the last gourd of water—saved from the previous day—before they went to bed. Each of them was saying the same thing to himself: "Tomorrow, those two *must* go down the mountain to get water!"

A day passed. No water. A second day went by. No water.

Nobody was out of bed when the fourth day arrived. The hall was deadly quiet, and so was the temple. No chanting, no beating rhythms on the wooden blocks. In the silent temple, a little mouse crawled up the drapery that covered the incense table. As he pulled himself up on to the tabletop, he bumped into a dish holding burning incense sticks, scattering them across the table and on to the floor. The draperies burst into flames, and soon the hall was full of smoke.

"Fire! Fire! Fire!" clamoured the young monk.

"Help! Help! Help!" cried the skinny monk.

"The buckets! Quick!" shouted the fat monk.

"Water!" yelled all three of them in unison.

The young monk grabbed the shoulder pole and two buckets and dashed to the mountain path. The skinny and the fat monks rushed into the hall. Choking and coughing, they peered through a sea of black smoke and saw the table blazing. Frantically, they stamped out the fire and dragged the smoking draperies out of the temple. As they hauled out the last one, a stubborn flame came to life again.

At that moment the young monk appeared, totally out of breath, his shoulder pole bowed by two buckets of water. Quickly, he poured the water on to the flame and rushed back to the stream. When he returned a second time, the skinny monk took over the shoulder pole, adjusted the buckets, and disappeared down the path.

That night, in the smoke-damaged hall, together, the three monks made a decision.

Early next morning, the three monks went down the mountainside and brought back a water vat. They installed it outside the temple. Carrying two buckets on his shoulder pole, the skinny monk scooted down and up the mountain to fill the vat with fresh water. The fat monk worked in the hall, moving out the smoke-damaged furniture, cleaning and fixing it.

And the young monk was totally absorbed in attending to the garden, straightening up the vegetables that had survived his neglect and planting some new ones.

A week later, when the three monks gathered at the brimming vat and drank fresh water, they looked at the garden, where the weeds had poked their green leaves out between the rows of vegetables.

The young monk slowly stood up and headed toward the garden. His two friends were close behind.

DIG DEEPER

1. Create a comic strip showing the main events in this story from the point of view of one of the three monks. Use speech balloons and thought bubbles to get across how and why the monk's thinking changed.

2. In a group, role-play a similar situation in a family. Show the consequences and a fair solution.

Connect and Share

You have read, viewed, and discussed many different stories about fairness and justice.

Now it's your turn to share ideas about fairness.

Tell a Story!

- Choose one of the stories you have read in this unit.

- Think about how to tell the story in your own words.

- Tell the story to a family member. Ask him or her what the story teaches about fairness.

Listen to a Story!

- Ask someone in your family to tell you a story about something in the past that wasn't fair. It could be a story from his or her own life or a story about an issue he or she has observed.

- Write down the story in your own words. Organize it into two parts: the past and today.

- Share it with a group in your class.

Spotlight on Learning

Collect

- Gather your notebooks, writing, and projects from this unit.

Talk and reflect

Work with a partner.

- Together, read the Learning Goals on page 2.
- Talk about how well you met these goals.
- Look through your work for evidence.

Select

- Choose two pieces of work that show how you achieved the Learning Goals. (The same piece of work can show more than one goal.)

Tell about your choices

- Tell why you chose each piece and what it shows about your learning.

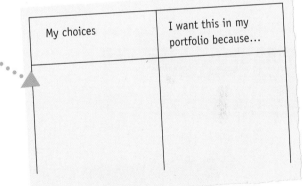

My choices	I want this in my portfolio because...

Reflect

- What have you learned about biographies and other ways of sharing events in someone's life?
- Which activities or selections had the biggest impact on your thinking about what is fair? Why?

61

Images
for Sale

LEARNING GOALS

In this unit you will

- View a variety of images from different media.

- Discover what happens behind the scenes in media production.

- Think critically about images you see.

- Use images and words to express your own point of view on a topic.

special effects (SFX)
computer-generated
imagery (CGi)
camera angle
storyboard
perspective
target audience

SPECIAL Effects

adapted by Chelsea Donaldson

How do directors create the images we see on screen?

Special effects (SFX) experts are the magicians who make movie and television scenes come to life.

Once a director decides what effect is needed, the special effects experts have to figure out how to make it happen. For example, they may be asked to create wild weather conditions, such as a snowstorm or a tornado, inside the film studio. How do they do it?

Blizzard!

The girl on the left looks like she is caught in the middle of a nasty blizzard. But as you can see in the wider shot above, she's really safe and sound inside a film studio. The "snow" under her feet is actually just plain salt. Those icicles in the corner of the window are moulded from plastic.

Creating this snowstorm in the film studio is a complicated process. One technician operates a machine that uses water and glycerine (a syrupy liquid) to create mist. Another technician piles bits of plastic and paper "snow" into a wind machine. Other specialists adjust the lighting to recreate the exact look of a stormy, snowy day.

A Window frame held in position by clamps
B Technician cranking a handle for extra "snow"
C Technician throwing extra "snow" in the background
D Technician operating a machine to make mist

Tornado Terror

In the old days, fog machines were sometimes used to create tornadoes for films. Today, however, computer-generated imagery (CGi) allows film crews to simulate awesome twisters with just a few clicks of the mouse. Using CGi, film clips of actual tornadoes can be combined with digital imagery. The result is terrifying scenes such as this one.

Electrifying Lightning

Lightning storms can be spectacular, but they are hard to capture on film. Instead, SFX wizards use computers to recreate the effect of forked lightning. The sounds of thunder are added later at a sound studio. Combined, these effects can produce storms that are even more impressive than the real thing!

Monsoon!

Not all special effects are created in the studio. Sometimes films are shot on location. Equipment, actors, and crew may have to be moved to other parts of the world. In the film scene shown above, the actors had to float down a river on a raft during a monsoon rainstorm. The sea was calm on the day of the shoot, but the film crew managed to create the effect of high winds and churning, stormy waters.

A Film crew revs boat's engine to create turbulence in the water
B Huge wind machines are used
C Waterproof cameras capture close-ups
D Sound engineer has to get close to the actors

LET'S TALK ABOUT IT...

- In your group, think of movies you have seen that use special effects. How did these techniques affect your reaction to the film?

- When might using technology to change or distort images be seen as inappropriate or even misleading?

Viewing Images

Images are all around us!

Think about a striking photograph, painting, or other image you have seen.

TALK ABOUT IT!

- Why did this image catch your attention?
- What makes you remember the image?
- Work with a partner. What types of images do you see
    - on the front page of a newspaper?
    - on the sports pages?
    - in fashion magazines?
    - in action movies?
    - on fan sites on the Internet?
    - in advertisements?

Make a chart together to show these types of images and their purpose.

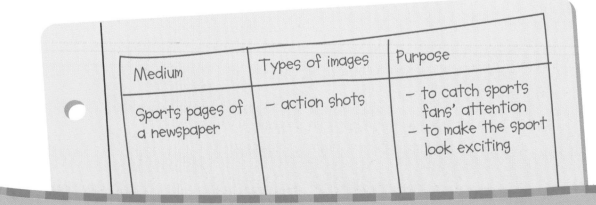

Medium	Types of images	Purpose
Sports pages of a newspaper	– action shots	– to catch sports fans' attention – to make the sport look exciting

Think Like a Viewer

Images have impact!

View with a purpose

- Why do you look at media images?

Crack the code

Here are some questions that will help you when you look at advertisements:

- How does the image make you feel?

- What specific techniques (e.g., lighting, camera angles) were used to create that feeling?

Make meaning

Practise using these strategies when you view media images:

USE WHAT YOU KNOW	What do you know about how images affect viewers? What other images does this one remind you of?
DECIDE WHAT'S IMPORTANT	Which parts of the image are most important? Why does the designer want you to notice them?
EVALUATE	Think about the message the designer is trying to send. How does the image help to get that message across?

Analyze what you see

- How does a designer decide what or whom to include in a media image?

- How does a designer decide what or who should *not* be included?

Fun Is a Phone Call Away

When it's time to make plans for after school or the weekend, make sure you don't get left out. With a C**ALL** *CONNECT* cell phone, you'll always know where to find friends and fun!

- Durable
- Keypad lights up in the dark
- Comes in a variety of colours

CALL CONNECT

Sometimes Good News Can't Wait

Don't wait to tell your latest news. It doesn't matter where you are or what you're doing. With a C**A**LL CONNECT cell phone, you can share your story with the people who matter most.

- Compact
- Clear digital sound from anywhere in the world
- Beeper alerts you to any missed messages

CALL CONNECT

Bringing Families Together

Talk every day with the people you care about. Whether they live across town, across the country, or across the ocean, a CALLCONNECT cell phone brings you together for all of life's important moments.

- Easy to use
- Clear digital sound from anywhere in the world
- Takes and sends pictures in seconds

CALL CONNECT

Reflect on Your Viewing

I thought it was interesting how the ads changed to target different people.

You have . . .

- viewed different advertisements for one product.
- noticed how advertisers can change the message to attract a different type of buyer.
- learned new vocabulary about creating media images.

special effects (SFX)

close-ups

film shoot

directors

computer-generated imagery (CGi)

You have also . . .

- explored different viewing strategies.

USE WHAT YOU KNOW

DECIDE WHAT'S IMPORTANT

EVALUATE

Write About Learning

Explain how the strategy "Decide what's important" helped you read the ads in "Who's the Audience?" How can you use this strategy when you view other media images?

View Like a Designer

Images can be combined with words to sell a product, present a point of view, or create a mood. The images and words in each ad in "Who's the Audience?" were designed to persuade a specific target audience.

HINT!

Think about the **target audience** for each image. The target audience is the group of people a media image is aimed at.

TALK ABOUT IT!

- What did you notice about how the text and images were similar in the ads? How were they different?

- How did the text and images appeal to you?

- With a group, make a list of how images are designed to persuade. What is it about the image that makes you want to buy the product?

Images that persuade
- are often combined with words
- show a particular point of view or perspective
- may create a certain mood or feeling
- try to make you look at the most important thing first

How can the opening credits of a TV show grab your interest?

Giving Credit

VIEW LIKE A DESIGNER

What does the designer's choice of images tell you about the show and its characters?

When you think about it, the opening credits of a TV show are like an ad for the show itself. Credits have to hook you and make you want to find out more. They should also tell you something about the show and its main characters— all in just 30 seconds!

Producers work with a creative director to design a show's opening credits. They start with a storyboard—a series of pictures that shows the sequence of scenes and how each scene will look.

On the following pages, you'll see a storyboard from a show called *Naturally, Sadie*. The main character is a young girl called Sadie Hawthorne. She enjoys observing wild animals and recording their behaviour. She also uses her powers of observation to record the behaviour of her family and friends!

At the bottom of each page, you'll see a colour image from the final version of the credits. Ideas often change, so you'll notice that the final images may be different from the pictures in the storyboard.

1 Open on Sadie sitting under a tree in a rain forest. Camera pushes in. She's wearing a backpack and has binoculars around her neck.

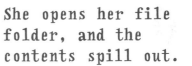

2 She opens her file folder, and the contents spill out.

The final version

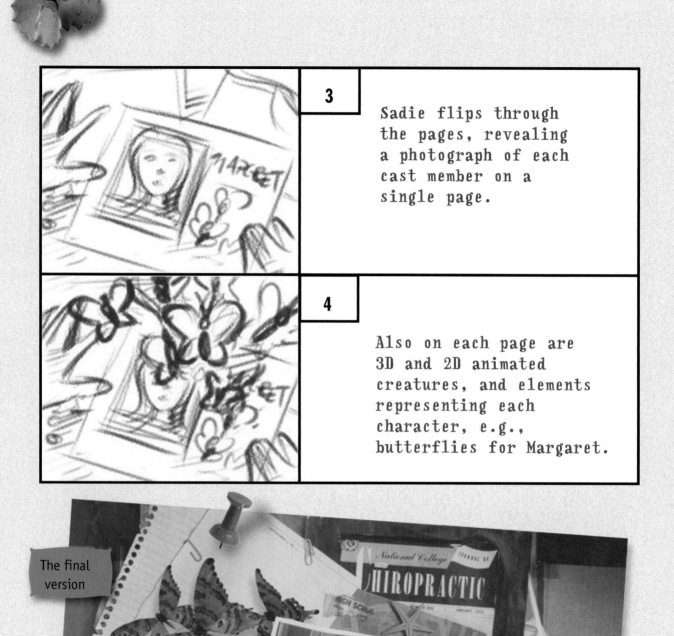

3	Sadie flips through the pages, revealing a photograph of each cast member on a single page.
4	Also on each page are 3D and 2D animated creatures, and elements representing each character, e.g., butterflies for Margaret.

The final version

(jasmine richards)
fig 1(c).

	5
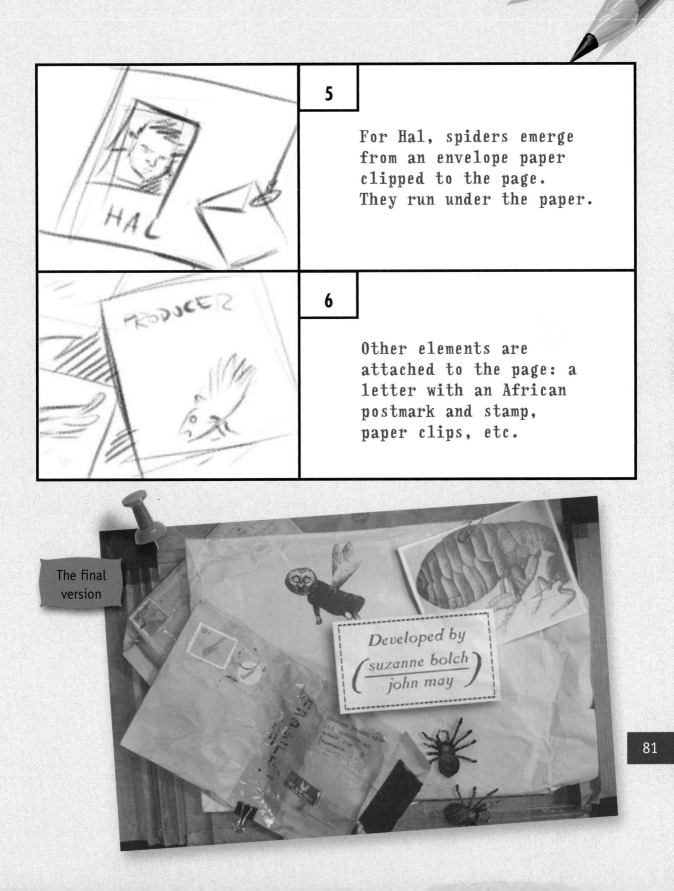	For Hal, spiders emerge from an envelope paper clipped to the page. They run under the paper.
	6
	Other elements are attached to the page: a letter with an African postmark and stamp, paper clips, etc.

The final version

Developed by
(suzanne bolch
john may)

| | **7** | Creative credits are handwritten names with animated hybrid animals. They'll look rubber stamped on the page. |
| | **8** | Camera pulls back to show Sadie in a vast rain forest. |

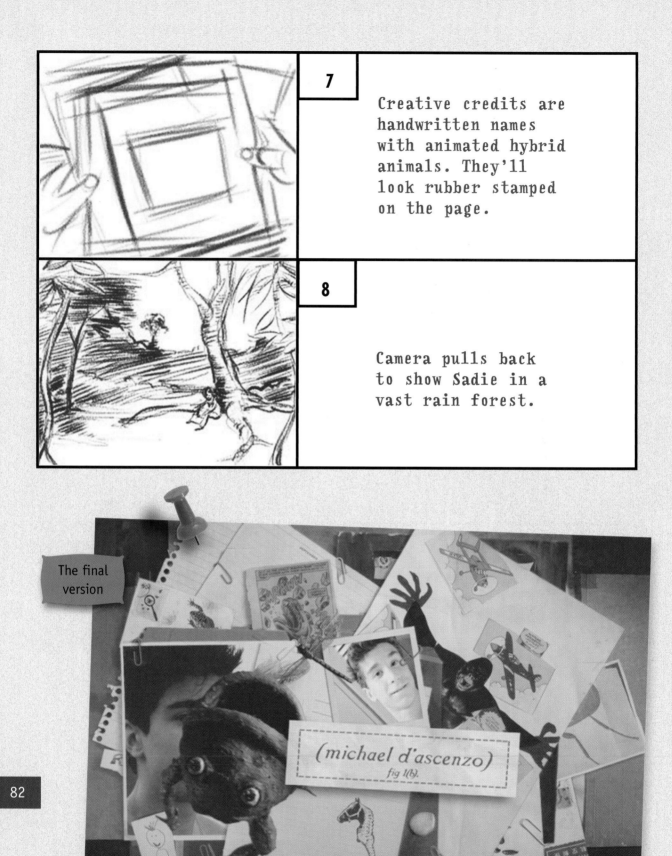

The final version

(michael d'ascenzo)
fig 1(b).

Meet the Artist

Craig Small is a creative director at an animation studio. He was responsible for creating and producing the Naturally, Sadie *opening credits. In an interview, Craig talked about his work.*

Craig Small

What process do you go through to create credits for a show?

The first step is to sit down with the client for a creative brief. This is a meeting where my client takes me through their ideas for the show and for the credits. The next step is to prepare a presentation. This usually involves the creation of storyboards. The storyboards are fine tuned until I get approval to proceed. Then we create a schedule for the job. We invite the client to view and comment on the job at key times during the process.

How did the idea for the *Naturally, Sadie* credits develop?

My first idea took the viewer through the eye of a microscope and into a sub-atomic world. The characters lived there with a host of strange creatures and weird environments. The producers of the show didn't feel that a microscope was the right tool for Sadie. They described her as a budding anthropologist who would observe her environment, not under a microscope but through binoculars. That description triggered an image I had seen of Jane Goodall. She was observing gorillas in the jungle with her notes on her lap. The producers loved the idea, and I took it from there.

MEDIA WATCH

Watch a trailer for a film you have already seen. How do the images capture the viewer's interest? Do they present an accurate image of the film? Why or why not?

DIG DEEPER

1. Based on the storyboard and images from *Naturally, Sadie*, what audience do you think the show is aimed at? How do you know?

2. In small groups, choose a TV show. Decide who the target audience is. Then brainstorm some creative ideas for the show's opening credits. Choose one idea and pitch it to another group. Be persuasive!

The TRUTH

Behind Those Perfect Pictures

Cover Up!

The Perfect Picture?

I was really excited when a teen media magazine called *Don't Buy It* asked me to be a cover model. *How hard can it be?* I thought. *After a haircut and a bit of touching up, I'll be ready, right?* Then I found out that those glamorous images you see in magazines take hours to create. Take a look at what I went through—**it's unreal!**

Smear, Slather, Spray...
Brr!

Modelling takes lots of time and gobs of glamour goo. The hair and makeup stylist spent nearly 2 hours and used more than 20 products to get me ready for the camera. Did you know that sometimes models have to soak their faces in freezing bowls of ice water to make their skin look "polished"?

Yikes!!!

VIEW LIKE A PHOTOGRAPHER
How do these photos support the idea that photographers can create unrealistic images?

Glamour goo!

2 hours later!!!

Over to the hair stylist...

There are 6 clothespins on the back of my shirt!

Pinch, Pull, Tuck—
Ouch!

My face, hair, and clothes were pulled in every direction. Modelling is hard work, and camera shoots involve many people who pay careful attention to details. For example, the wardrobe stylist used clothespins to smooth and tuck fabric that wasn't lying right!

Help! I'm Disappearing!

Photographers typically take hundreds of pictures during a shoot just so they can get one best shot for a magazine cover. Once the photo is chosen, it is sent to the graphics department to be touched up on computer.

AFTER

BEFORE

Wait until you see what they did to me here!

They touched up my hair, the side of my face, my eyes, my skin, AND my teeth! What was wrong with the way I was?

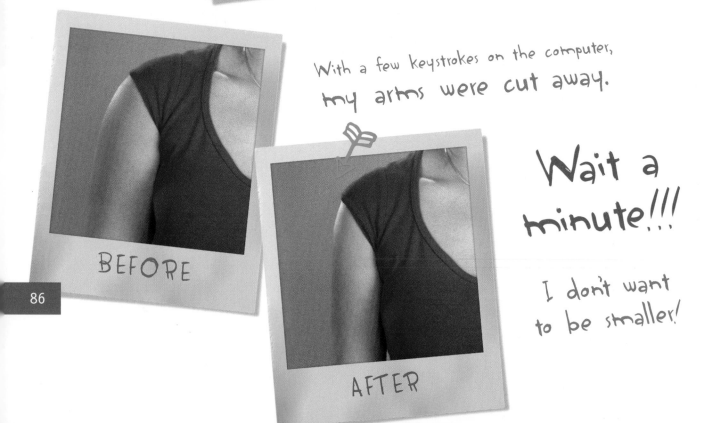

BEFORE

AFTER

With a few keystrokes on the computer, my arms were cut away.

Wait a minute!!!

I don't want to be smaller!

The Cover Image: Where's the real me gone?

Don't Buy It

Cover Up!
The Truth Behind Those Perfect Pictures

How DO they get those special effects?

and much, much more...

It was fun being a model for a day. But no matter how many beauty products I buy, it's going to be impossible to look like a cover model in real life. And that's okay! Always wearing clothespins and keeping a bunch of stylists with me at all times? Now that's not a perfect picture!

Do you recognize me? I don't!

DIG DEEPER

1. What messages do retouched media images of models send to girls about how they should look or act? Write a short journal entry explaining how you or people you know are affected by these messages.

2. Look through sports or fashion magazines for images of men that you think have been touched up. Discuss what message these images might send to boys your age about how they should look or act.

Look at four or five covers from different editions of the same magazine. What do the covers tell you about the magazine and its target audience?

What
Do You SEE on TV?

by Shelagh Wallace

How can TV images present a point of view?

Look around the room you're in. Now, cup your hands around your eyes as though you're holding a pair of binoculars. Look around the room again. As you look through the frame you've made, you see certain parts of the room at a time, and you view them from your own unique position. You are seeing things from your point of view.

Like your cupped hands, a television screen frames what you see on TV and gives you a certain view of the show's sets, the actors, and the action. But unlike the things you see through your cupped hands, the pictures on your screen don't have your point of view. Instead, you're watching a point of view that was chosen by the directors to make you pay attention to what they have decided is important in the show. The directors also want you to react in specific ways to what you see—they want you to cheer the show's hero, but not the bad guy—so they use a number of tricks to make this happen.

Cameras shooting a scene in a TV studio

Get the Right Angle

Directors have lots of choices when it comes to picking the angle the camera will shoot from. A high-angle shot can make whatever's being photographed look small or less important because it's shot from above. This shot gives you, the viewer, a feeling of power because you seem larger than what you're looking at.

High-angle shots can also show you something the characters can't see and, for this reason, are used to build suspense in detective shows and mysteries. For example, when you see detectives in the deserted warehouse far below, moving unknowingly straight towards the crooks, you know that they're headed for trouble before *they* do.

The opposite kind of shot, a low-angle shot, is taken from below an object and looks up at it. It makes whatever's being photographed look larger and more important than the viewer. For instance, a knee-level shot emphasizes how tall the building is and how short you are by comparison.

This **high-angle shot** gives you a view that people on the floor don't have. It shows the excitement on the athletes' faces and how close the ball is to the net!

This **low-angle shot** helps you imagine you are there—you can *feel* the height and majesty of the skyscrapers.

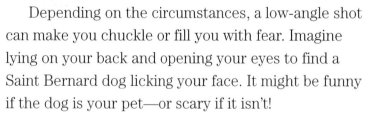

VIEW LIKE A DIRECTOR
How does the camera angle in each of the photographs affect your response?

Low-angle shots
can be very amusing!

An **eye-level shot** presents a simple, straightforward view of the subject.

Depending on the circumstances, a low-angle shot can make you chuckle or fill you with fear. Imagine lying on your back and opening your eyes to find a Saint Bernard dog licking your face. It might be funny if the dog is your pet—or scary if it isn't!

A "normal" or eye-level shot is used most of the time, in most TV shows. It's the same angle at which people usually look at each other, so it's a familiar, comfortable angle for viewing things. Unlike high-angle and low-angle shots, an eye-level shot doesn't "comment" at all on what's being photographed.

Go the Distance

By changing the distance between the camera and whatever's being photographed, a director can also direct your attention to whatever he or she wants you to see. A long (or wide) shot has a lot of distance between the camera and what you see. This shot gives you a sense of the "big picture" or situation. It's also called an "establishing shot" whenever it's used at the beginning of a scene to establish the general setting. Look for it at the beginning of a sitcom, right after the credits: it's usually the shot of the character's house or apartment building where most of the action takes place. Different kinds of shows have different establishing shots. On a talk show, for instance, this shot might include the whole stage and the audience.

A **long shot** lets you see the big picture.

The background in a **medium shot** can provide a lot of information. What clues in this photo tell you that this man is a news anchor?

A medium shot has less distance between the camera and an object than a wide shot. In this kind of shot, the persons or objects you're looking at are just as important as what's behind them. (You will usually see a person from the chest up.) Most shots on TV are medium shots.

A close-up shot moves in very close and directs your attention to an object or a person. Look for close-up shots on talk shows and soap operas, especially when the actors or talk-show guests are talking about a highly emotional topic. Directors rely on a lot of close-ups to keep you so involved with the people on TV that you'll continue to watch their program.

Another kind of close-up shot, the extreme close-up, isn't used very often on TV. If you do see this kind of shot, it will probably be in a scary movie. Seeing a huge eyeball right up close, for example, can really startle and shock you!

A **close-up shot** is great for showing emotions!

An **extreme close-up shot** can be very scary!

EEK!

Now Comes the Hard Part!

After taping and during editing, the director makes the final decision about which camera shots will be used in the show. And there can be lots of shots to choose from! Most sitcoms, for example, are taped twice in front of an audience and then twice without an audience. Three or four cameras, each at a different angle and distance, are used each time as the scenes are shot out of sequence. After taping, the very best shots are selected and pieced together in the correct order, a process that can take up to 50 hours for a single half-hour episode.

Now that you know more about what you see on your TV, you'll probably spot camera angles, effects, and other techniques that you've never noticed before. Why are the directors using a certain camera effect? How do you react when you see the effect? What else is going on, and should you accept everything you see at first glance? Finding out the answers to these questions is part of the fun of being a tuned-in TV watcher and really seeing what's on TV!

TV TIDBIT

After a TV show has been shot and edited, any problems with the dialogue are corrected, and music and sound effects are added. Directors refer to this process as "sweetening."

DIG DEEPER

1. Choose one camera angle and explain to a friend how it enhances the images we see. Suggest other situations where a photographer might want to use this type of shot.

2. With a partner, look through newspapers to find three images that show specific camera angles. For each image, write a caption describing the angle and the effect it creates.

Producers at Work!

Images can be very powerful. Producers use storyboards to plan the images they will use.

Plan a Slide Show Documentary

- Brainstorm ideas for a short slide show documentary about one aspect of your school.
- Decide what message you want to send about your school.
- Decide who your target audience will be (e.g., new students, parents, your class members).

IDEAS TO TRY
Your documentary could focus on a school sports team, a club, or the history of the school.

Make a Storyboard

- Create a storyboard to show what your documentary will look like.
- Decide what images you could use.
- What types of shots and camera angles will you use to emphasize your message?
- How will you grab the viewers' interest?

Write a Script

- Write words to go with each image in your slide show.
- Decide on a title for your documentary.

PRESENTATION POINTER
Think about what you *don't* want to include. Don't include images or information that is off topic or sends a different message from the one you are trying to get across.

Slide Show Storyboard:
Renton Memorial Public School — Then and Now!

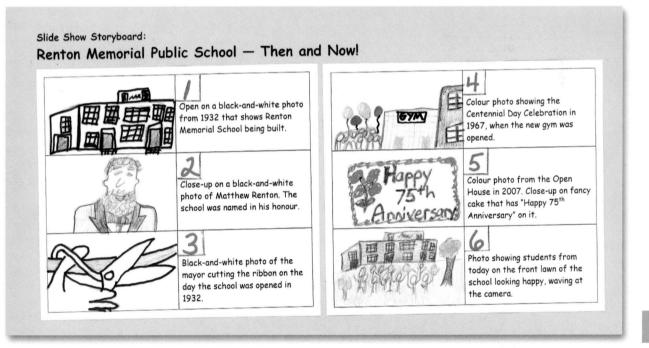

1. Open on a black-and-white photo from 1932 that shows Renton Memorial School being built.

2. Close-up on a black-and-white photo of Matthew Renton. The school was named in his honour.

3. Black-and-white photo of the mayor cutting the ribbon on the day the school was opened in 1932.

4. Colour photo showing the Centennial Day Celebration in 1967, when the new gym was opened.

5. Colour photo from the Open House in 2007. Close-up on fancy cake that has "Happy 75th Anniversary" on it.

6. Photo showing students from today on the front lawn of the school looking happy, waving at the camera.

Born to Stand Out!

by Breanna Myles

What makes you stand out?

Trying to fit in
Blend in and about
The problem with this
You were born to stand out

Afraid to be different
In fear and in shame
But here you are wrong
Cuz no two are the same

The media frames us
Saying what we should be
But why don't they get it
I just want to be me

READ LIKE A WRITER

How does the poet use repetition and rhyme to highlight important ideas?

Blonde, thin and beautiful
Trying to be like everyone else
But at the same time
I am losing myself

What if no one likes the real me
As you ask in doubt
But don't be afraid
You were born to stand out

It's time to breakaway
That's what life is about
So let go of your fears
You were born to stand out

DIG DEEPER

1. This poem was written by a young teen. What do you think the poet means when she says that "The media frames us / Saying what we should be"?

2. How do media images affect you? Express your ideas in a collage, a poem, or some other medium.

Brand Names

adapted from *Zillions Magazine*

Are brand names really worth paying extra for?

Can you tell which is the expensive brand-name outfit and which is the bargain look-alike?

We shopped around for big-brand clothes and less expensive look-alikes. Then we hid all the labels and logos to see if kids could tell which was which.

Can YOU tell the difference? Guess which outfit in each pair is the one with the big brand names—and the big price tag!

Outfit 1
Red-striped polo shirt
White cotton T-shirt
Blue jeans

vs. Look-Alikes

Outfit 2

White jeans
Light blue tank top
Denim jacket

VIEW LIKE A PHOTOGRAPHER
How has the photographer made
the clothes look desirable?

99

Outfit 3

Black top with cap sleeves
Cargo army pants

So, What's the Deal?
Could you tell the difference?

Many kids mistake look-alikes for name brands. In fact, most people find it difficult to tell the difference between brand-name clothes and their look-alikes. They like them both.

Clothing look-alikes are no coincidence. Companies actually track big-brand styles, copy them, and sell them for less. A designer for one such company told us that most clothes "are knock-offs of expensive designer clothes that sold well."

So the next time a big-brand garment catches your eye, shop around. Its look-alike might be just around the corner, selling for a whole lot less!

DIG DEEPER

1. Before you look at the answers, write down which outfits you think are brand-name clothes. Then check to see how many of your responses are correct. Compare your results with those of other class members. Show the results in a graph or chart.

2. Why do you think some people are willing to spend more for brand-name clothing? Create a list of guidelines for being a smart consumer.

Answer Key
Outfit 1: Brand name on the right ($165 vs. $68)
Outfit 2: Brand name on the right ($528 vs. $125)
Outfit 3: Brand name on the left ($178 vs. $60)

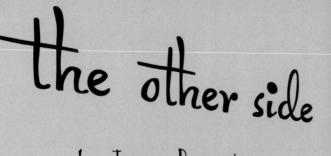

the other side

by Istvan Banyai

the other side

by Istvan Banyai

How can seeing things from a different perspective change our understanding?

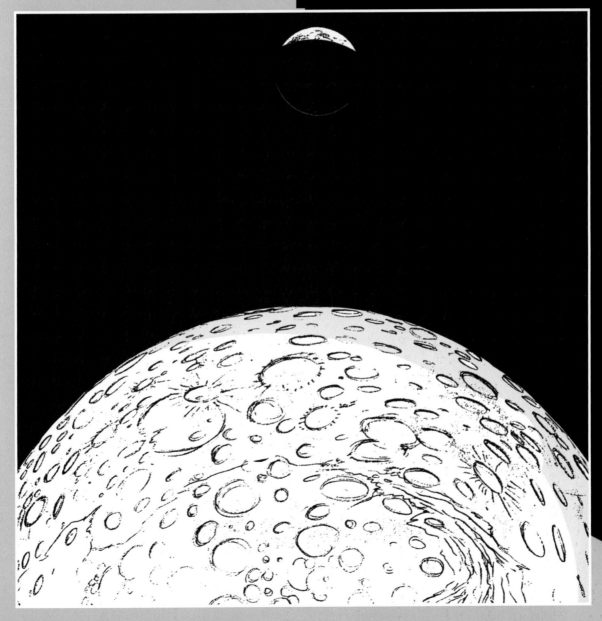

VIEW LIKE AN ARTIST
In each pair of images, how does the artist change the mood of the scene by changing the perspective?

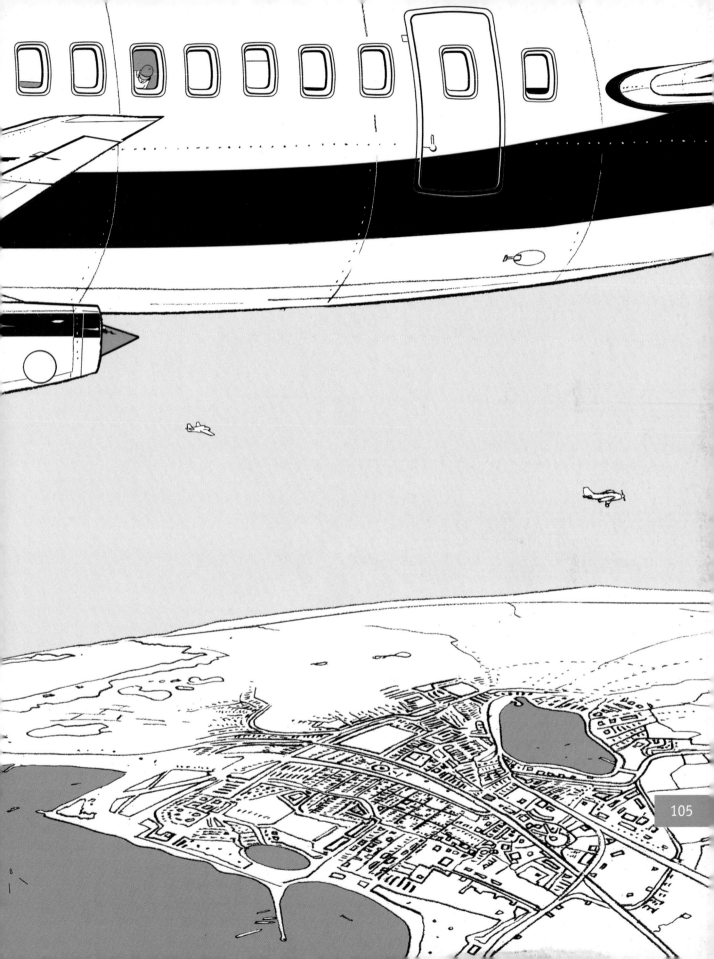

DIG DEEPER ·······························

1. For each pair of images, discuss with a partner how your understanding of the scene was changed by viewing it from a different perspective.

2. Why is it important to look at things from more than one perspective? Discuss with a partner. Express your ideas in a short poem, a reflective paragraph, or a pair of images.

A Tangled Web

by Sara Snow and Susin Nielsen

How much power can one image have?

This script is from a television series that follows the story of Cree teenager Jack Sinclair and his best friend Zoey Jones. They are the co-founders of an online teen magazine. In this excerpt, Jack and Zoey find out just how powerful images can be—especially when they are posted on the Internet.

Crystal Sinclair

Sandi Bhutella

Jack Sinclair

Zoey Jones

JACK'S HOUSE - BASEMENT - EVENING 1

On a computer—a video-clip of FRANCINE singing (off-tune)
a pop song of Francine's own creation, complete with an
awkward dance.

READ LIKE A WRITER
How do the scriptwriters help
you visualize the scenes?

FRANCINE ON SCREEN *(singing)*
You are my love/Like a wounded dove/Someone above/To heal my
wounds/Bring me balloons...

She mimes catching balloons that are floating by.

REVEAL—JACK and ZOEY watching this. They're both smiling,
but Zoey's smile is wider. She finally breaks into laughter.

ZOEY
Where'd you get this?

JACK
She e-mailed it—said we could put it on the joke page if we thought
it was funny enough.

ZOEY *(nods)*
It's hilarious.

*Francine finishes her clumsy but exuberant dance with a final
pose, and the clip ends. Zoey laughs and gets up.*

ZOEY
Check me out.

She imitates a couple of Francine's dance moves.

JACK *(laughing)*
Canadian Idol, here you come!

*Zoey smiles and gives him a whack on the shoulder. Fending her
off, Jack clicks the mouse a few times.*

JACK

Welcome to our Web site, Francine. You're gonna get a ton of laughs.

ZOEY

Can you play it again?

JACK

Sure.

Jack clicks the mouse, and they smile with anticipation.

PUSH IN—to a CLOSE-UP of Francine on the computer.

SCHOOL - GYM HALLWAY - DAY 2

Francine heads down the hall and notices a few STUDENTS glance her way and laugh. She comes upon CRYSTAL.

CRYSTAL *(smiles)*

Hey, Francine. I gotta admit you've got way more guts than I do.

FRANCINE

What do you mean?

Crystal motions further down the hall, and Francine sees A FEW STUDENTS watching SEAN as he imitates Francine's video clip.

SEAN *(bad singing)*

You are my love/a wounded dove/someone above/heal my wounds/
bring balloons.

Sean mimes catching balloons and finishes in the same
pose Francine did, inciting gales of laughter from the students.
Francine recognizes the song and dance, but stares in shock.

FRANCINE
I don't get it.

CRYSTAL
It's on my brother's Web site.

FRANCINE
What's on your brother's Web site?

CRYSTAL
You—singing that song.

Francine's expression turns to dread.

SCHOOL - COMMON AREA - DAY 2

Francine finds Jack doing homework at one of the tables.

> FRANCINE
> Jack?

Jack looks up and recognizes her right away.

> JACK *(smiles)*
> Hey, Francine. Your clip's perfect for the joke page.
> It's getting tons of hits.

> FRANCINE
> Can you please take it off your Web site?

> JACK *(taken aback)*
> What?!

> FRANCINE
> Everyone's laughing at me.

> JACK
> You sent it to the joke page.

> FRANCINE
> I didn't send it.

> JACK
> But it came on your e-mail.

> FRANCINE
> I didn't send it.

ON Jack—as it sinks in.

FRANCINE
Please. Can you just make it go away?

JACK *(nods)*
Sure.

Francine walks off as Jack watches her.

THE UNDERGROUND - DAY 2
Jack at a computer as Crystal watches him clicking the mouse. Jack sits back.

JACK
There—Francine is off the Net.

CRYSTAL
You wouldn't believe how many people saw it.

JACK
Really?

Crystal nods. Jack shrugs to suggest he doesn't get it.

JACK
Yeah, well. It's over now.

DOLLY TO—a couple of STUDENTS on another computer viewing another Web site. One of the students clicks an icon and we see Francine's video come up on screen. The student clicks the mouse again and leans back, and we see Francine's video play.

FRANCINE ON SCREEN *(singing)*
You are my love/Like a wounded dove/Someone above/To heal my wounds/Bring me balloons...

The students laugh as Francine dances.

SCHOOL - COMMON AREA - DAY 3
Francine tries to go quickly past a GROUP of students, but she's noticed immediately. The group murmurs, and four of them break into song and dance, mimicking her video while the rest clap and cheer at her. Humiliated, Francine picks up her pace and moves on.

SCHOOL - HALLWAY #3 DAY 3
Francine approaches her locker, then stops and stares at it from a distance.

REVEAL—Francine's locker with several balloons taped to the door.

Francine just stands, staring at it.

SCHOOL - MULTI-PURPOSE ROOM - DAY 3

Jack and Sandi sit in front of a computer and glance at Zoey as she makes her way towards them. As she puts down the tapes, she sees what they're looking at—a doctored version of Francine's video clip. Someone has gone through the trouble of adding balloons and putting a sparkly dress on Francine.

FRANCINE ON SCREEN *(singing)*

Zoey can't believe it. Jack's looking glum.

ZOEY
What happened?

JACK
Other Web sites downloaded it from our site before I took it off.

SANDI
Yeah, and they added some really cool effects.

JACK
It's getting way out of control.

ZOEY
Some people have way too much time on their hands.

SANDI *(singing)*
You are my love, like a wounded dove...

Jack and Zoey turn and give Sandi a look. He stops.

SANDI
Sorry.

Jack shakes his head and exits the Web site.

SCHOOL - HALLWAY #3 - DAY 3
Jack strides up to Crystal, who closes her locker.

JACK
How's Francine doing?

CRYSTAL
Not very good.

She motions to more balloons attached to Francine's locker and a picture of Francine drawn on her locker. Jack winces.

CRYSTAL
Every time she took them down, some other kid put more up.

JACK
You know where I can find her?

CRYSTAL
She's probably at home. She's thinking about switching
to another school.

JACK
What!?

Crystal nods.

END

1. In this excerpt, whoever e-mailed the video to Jack is never caught or punished. If you could talk to this person, what would you say to bring home the seriousness of his or her actions? What consequences do you think this person should face? Discuss with a partner.

2. Could this incident have been prevented? With a partner, create a poster or design a Web page to persuade students to take precautions before posting or downloading images.

Connect and Share

Ads contain some of the most striking images you'll see. They try to grab your attention and make you take notice.

Now it's your turn to talk about ad images that catch your eye.

Watch a show together!

- Choose a half-hour television show to watch with a family member.
- Whenever an ad comes on, discuss it with your family member. Which images in the ads did you find most striking? Why? Whom do you think the ad was meant to target?
- Keep a record sheet like the one shown below.

Share your ideas!

- Choose one image from the ads that you liked or found interesting. In a small group, describe the image and explain why you chose it. Explain whether your family member felt the same way.

DESCRIBING IMAGES

When you are describing the images you see in ads, consider how the advertiser uses these techniques:

- contrast
- humour or surprise
- camera angles
- colour

Most of the ads I liked were funny. My dad liked those ads, too.

Watching Ads

Ads I saw	Images I liked	My family member's reaction

Spotlight on Learning

Collect

- Gather your notebooks, your writing, and other work you did in this unit.

Talk and reflect

Work with a partner.

- Together, read the Learning Goals on page 62.
- Talk about how well you met these goals.
- Look through your work for evidence.

Select

- Choose two pieces of work that show how you achieved the Learning Goals. (The same piece of work can show more than one goal.)

Tell about your choices

- Tell why you chose each piece and what it shows about your learning.

My choices	I want this in my portfolio because...

Reflect

- What have you learned about viewing and creating images?
- Explain one interesting media technique you learned about or explored.

The Wonders of Space

LEARNING GOALS

In this unit you will

- Read, view, and listen to fiction and non-fiction texts about space.

- Make connections to what you already know and wonder about space.

- Use scientific terms to describe and explain information and ideas.

- Research and present information about space using diagrams, visuals, and headings.

atmosphere
planet
meteor
extraterrestrial
telescope
astronomy

SPACE
A GUIDED TOUR

What would it be like to visit the planets?

Have you ever visualized going on a visit to the planets? Think how exciting it would be to zoom to Neptune, journey to Jupiter, or watch the stars from Mars. Of course, humans are not yet able to arrange vacations to outer space. So, in the meantime, here's a sampling of what you might see if you could take a guided tour of our solar system.

MERCURY

It would be difficult to know what to pack to visit Mercury. During the day, the temperature is hot enough to melt metal, but at night it plunges to a bone-chilling, teeth-chattering cold. The temperature changes wildly from day to night because there is very little atmosphere. The atmosphere is the mix of gases surrounding a planet, and it acts like a big blanket, trapping the Sun's heat. When there's very little atmosphere, heat escapes easily.

Craters on Mercury make this planet look quite similar to the moon.

MERCURY DATA

Moons: 0	Rings: 0	Distance from Sun: 57 909 175 km

VENUS

Venus, our closest neighbour, is scorching hot, so you would have to put on powerful sunglasses and turn on the cosmic air conditioning just to fly by. It's certainly no place for people! Venus is the hottest planet, even though it is not the closest one to the Sun. Venus's thick, cloudy atmosphere traps the Sun's heat most effectively.

Although Venus is blazing hot, it would be beautiful to view. Imagine a place with an orange sky and yellow clouds. Those swirling clouds may look lovely, but they are made of poisonous gas.

VENUS DATA

| Moons: 0 | Rings: 0 | Distance from Sun: 108 208 930 km |

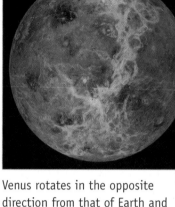

Venus rotates in the opposite direction from that of Earth and the other planets. On Venus, therefore, the Sun rises in the west and sets in the east.

MARS

Up close, Mars looks like a red jewel because its surface is covered in a red dust that contains iron. It may look like a hot desert, but the temperature's always cold, even during the day.

Mars is much like Earth. It has ice caps on the north and south poles; huge canyons; broad, flat plains; and even volcanoes. However, the Martian atmosphere is very different from Earth's since it contains carbon dioxide, which is the gas humans breathe out.

MARS DATA

| Moons: 2 | Rings: 0 | Distance from Sun: 227 936 640 km |

The largest volcano in the solar system, Olympus Mons, is on Mars. It is three times taller than Mount Everest.

123

On the next part of your imaginary tour, you would pass Earth and blast through the asteroid belt to reach the outer planets. You couldn't land on them because they are balls of gas. But here's what you might see as you whizzed by.

JUPITER

Jupiter is wrapped in bands of pink, yellow, red, tan, and white clouds. Strong winds and the planet's spin stretch the clouds into strips of colour. Jupiter has a giant red spot. The spot is a hurricane that has been raging for over 300 years!

Jupiter is so large that all the other planets in the solar system could fit inside it.

JUPITER DATA

Moons: 63	Rings: 3	Distance from Sun: 778 412 020 km

SATURN

Saturn is a lovely lemon-yellow colour and beautiful to look at, but don't get too close! The winds in the upper atmosphere are five times faster than the strongest hurricane-force winds on Earth. Saturn's rings are made of billions of chunks of ice, dust, and rock. These chunks can be smaller than a grain of sand or larger than a house.

Saturn's largest moon, Titan, is bigger than Mercury.

SATURN DATA

Moons: 46	Rings: 7	Distance from Sun: 1 426 725 400 km

URANUS

The gas in the atmosphere of Uranus makes the planet a beautiful blue-green colour. Uranus lies on its side. Astronomers think this planet might have been hit by a large object that knocked it over.

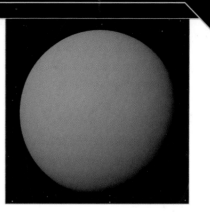

Most of Uranus's moons are named after people in plays written by William Shakespeare.

URANUS DATA

Moons: 27	Rings: 11	Distance from Sun: 2 870 972 200 km

NEPTUNE

Neptune might look big and blue like a tropical ocean, but it's not warm. Like all of the gas planets, it's freezing cold. Its strong winds and speedy rotation make Neptune one of the stormiest planets in our solar system.

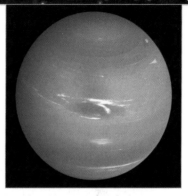

It takes Neptune more than 160 years to orbit the Sun.

NEPTUNE DATA

Moons: 13	Rings: 4	Distance from Sun: 4 498 252 900 km

LET'S TALK ABOUT IT...

- With a partner, review the descriptions in this selection. Then choose a planet you would both like to visit. Explain your choice to another pair.

- Use your imagination to role-play a scene in which you visit one of the planets. Work in a group to present your role play to the class. (You can make your scene funny or scary if you like.)

Reading in Science

Reading and viewing in science help you get information about our world—and beyond!

TALK ABOUT IT!

Think about a science book, article, or Web site you have used to find information about space.

- What topic were you researching?

- What did you find most useful about the resource?

- Tell a partner something you learned from this resource.

Here are some places you can find information about space.

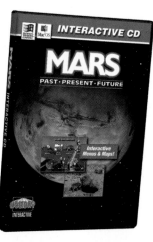

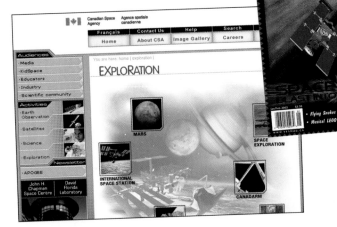

Make a chart together to show features that make a resource useful for research.

Features of a Useful Science Resource

Feature	What makes it useful
– photographs with captions	– I can see what the objects really look like.

Think Like a Reader

Read with a purpose

- Why do you read about science topics such as space?

Crack the code

When you see technical terms and difficult words in science, look for parts of the word you already know.

uni)verse

atmo(sphere)

(astro)naut

tele(scope)

Make meaning

Practise using these strategies when you are reading in science:

ASK QUESTIONS	Think about what you already know about the topic. Ask questions about what you would like to know.
PAUSE AND CHECK	Pause at the end of each paragraph or section to check your understanding.
SUMMARIZE	Organize the important information in a web or other graphic form.

Analyze what you read

- Why might two experts give you different answers to the same question about space?

- Does information about space ever change? Why or why not?

Space Rocks

Space is far from empty. It contains rocks of all sizes—from tiny particles to giant boulders.

Space rocks have collided with our planet in the past. Could collisions happen again?

ASK QUESTIONS

What would you like to learn about space rocks?

What Are Space Rocks?

Space rocks are objects left over from the time our solar system was formed 4.6 billion years ago. The three main types of space rocks are comets, asteroids, and meteoroids.

- Comets are sometimes called "dirty snowballs." They are made of ice, dust, and rock.

- Asteroids are rocks that orbit the Sun. They range in size from small boulders to 1000 km–wide giants.

- Meteoroids are small pieces of asteroids or comets. They are called meteors (or shooting stars) when they enter Earth's atmosphere. If they land, they are called meteorites.

How Do They Collide with Earth?

Like planets, space rocks orbit the Sun. Most of them travel far from Earth. But some have orbits that bring them near Earth's path around the Sun. Some scientists call them "Earth-crossing objects" because their orbits cross Earth's orbit. As they cross, some of the rocks fall through the atmosphere and hit Earth's surface.

PAUSE AND CHECK

What have you learned about space rocks so far? Does it make sense?

Why Are They Dangerous?

Sometimes an object crashes into Earth leaving a large crater behind. Once every few million years, a collision occurs that is so catastrophic, it changes everything on Earth, even the climate! Scientists believe that this kind of impact caused the extinction of dinosaurs millions of years ago. Today researchers are working on plans to track and intercept large objects before they reach Earth's surface.

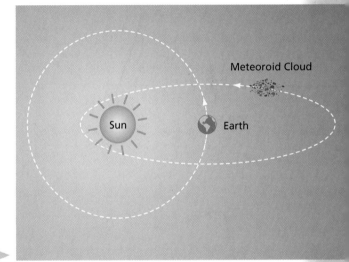

Some space rocks cross Earth's orbit around the Sun. ▶

Some Large Impact Craters in Canada

Crater Name	Location	Age (Years)	Diameter
Sudbury	Ontario	1.85 billion	250 km
Manicouagan	Quebec	212 million	100 km
Montagnais	Nova Scotia	50 million	45 km
Saint Martin	Manitoba	220 million	40 km
Carswell	Saskatchewan	115 million	39 km
Steen River	Alberta	95 million	25 km

SUMMARIZE

Organize the information you have read in a web or other graphic form.

Space Junk

This piece of a rocket crashed into a field in Texas.

ASK QUESTIONS

What would you like to learn about space junk?

We have sent satellites, spacecraft, and other equipment into space. What happens to these things once they leave Earth?

What Is Space Junk?

Space junk is the name for everything that humans have left in space. That includes objects as tiny as flecks of paint and as large as a whole spacecraft. Scientists estimate that there are millions of pieces of space junk orbiting Earth, including old satellites, rocket bodies, and trash from space missions.

130

How Is Space Junk Created?

Some objects that we send into space cause no problems. For example, scientists control space shuttles from Earth to make sure they come back safely. Many items, however, are just left in orbit. Over time, they fall apart. They may collide with each other and explode into smaller pieces.

Why Is Space Junk a Problem?

Most pieces of space junk are tiny, but they are moving at extremely fast speeds. At 40 000 km/h, even a fleck of paint can damage the window on a space shuttle. A larger object striking a satellite could cause it to fail.

At times, space junk can even come crashing back to Earth. Scientists think that about 1400 tonnes of space junk have fallen from the sky. Smaller objects burn up when they hit Earth's atmosphere. The pieces that survive tend to be large and heavy, so they cause an impact when they land. The largest piece of junk to hit Earth was the Russian Space Station *Mir*, which landed safely in the Pacific Ocean in 2001.

PAUSE AND CHECK

What have you learned about space junk so far? Does it make sense?

This model shows space junk in Earth's orbit. Each dot represents one object. The circle in the centre represents Earth.

Examples of Space Junk Crashes

Year	Location	Description
1978	NWT, Canada	metal fragments from Russian satellite
1994	Mexico	20 kg metal plate from Russian satellite
2000	South Africa	270 kg metal sphere from U.S. rocket
2004	Brazil	30 kg metal object from U.S. rocket

SUMMARIZE

Organize the information you have read in a web or other graphic form.

Extraterrestrial Life

Tube worms like these can live in extreme conditions on Earth. Could similar life forms survive on other planets?

ASK QUESTIONS

What would you like to learn about extraterrestrial life?

For as long as people have been looking into space, they have been wondering whether life exists anywhere else in the universe.

What Is Extraterrestrial Life?

Extraterrestrial life is the term scientists use for living things that could survive beyond Earth's environment. So far, the only life we know about in the universe exists on Earth. But scientists believe that extraterrestrial life may exist somewhere very far away.

132

Is There Life Beyond Earth?

Scientists have made recent discoveries that suggest life may be possible elsewhere in the universe. Three recent developments in science are especially important.

- Scientists have discovered living things in places where they once thought life could not survive. Living things have been found inside volcanoes and in the deep ocean. Perhaps they exist in space, as well.

- Planets outside our solar system have been discovered. Conditions needed for life might exist there.

- There is now evidence that all matter in the universe—including our solar system and all life on Earth—was created at the same time and in the same way.

How Can We Search for Signs of Life?

Scientists rely on space technologies, such as telescopes and space probes, to gather information and send it back to Earth. These tools may someday help to prove that life exists elsewhere in the universe.

PAUSE AND CHECK

What have you learned about extraterrestrial life so far? Does it make sense?

These radio telescopes, in British Columbia, are searching the skies for signs of extraterrestrial life.

Tools for Finding Extraterrestrial Life

Technology	Function
Deep space probes	Carry instruments that collect information about space
Planet-finding telescopes	Orbit Earth and scan the skies for new planets
Radio telescopes	Listen for radio signals from space that might be coming from intelligent life
Remote-controlled rovers	Move across a planet's surface and gather information

SUMMARIZE

Organize the information you have read in a web or other graphic form.

133

Reflect on Your Reading

You have . . .

- talked about what is out in space.
- read and viewed information about space.
- learned new vocabulary and scientific terms about space.

extraterrestrial life

comet

asteroid

meteoroid

space probe

radio telescope

space junk

I can imagine life on other planets. Can you?

You have also . . .

- explored different reading strategies.

ASK QUESTIONS

PAUSE AND CHECK

SUMMARIZE

134

Write About Learning

Information about science is constantly changing. Until recently, Pluto was considered a planet in our solar system. If you read science information that tells about Pluto as a planet, you will know that the information is out of date. Write about how you know if a source is current and reliable.

Read Like a Writer

When you were reading "What's Out There?" you were reading *explanations*. Explanations try to answer questions in the clearest way possible.

TALK ABOUT IT!

- How does the writer make the topics interesting?

- How does the writer organize the information?

- What special features did you notice?

HINT!

Think about how the writer **organizes** the information to help the reader understand.

How Writers Organize Explanations

- use headings to organize ideas

- illustrate ideas with photos or diagrams

- use tables or charts to organize details or numbers

- use captions to link visuals with the text

Space Tomatoes!

by Elizabeth MacLeod
Illustrated by Kevin Cheng

How might space affect the way plants grow?

Can you imagine eating only dried food, or food in bags or tubes, for almost three years? That's how long it would take to fly to Mars and back. Providing astronauts with tasty, nutritious food is one of the biggest challenges facing the space program.

One option is to have astronauts grow their own food as they zoom to other planets. Growing food on a spacecraft would save storage space on board and would lighten the load for liftoff. But if scientists are going to send seeds into space, they need to know which types of plants will grow, stay healthy, and produce the biggest crop. To find this information, researchers started the Tomatosphere project and asked students in Grades 3 to 10 for help.

READ LIKE A WRITER
How does the writer use questions to organize the information?

These students are part of the Tomatosphere project. They are measuring some tomato plants that they grew in their classroom.

137

Classrooms across Canada participated in the Tomatosphere project. This poster shows students who helped astronauts find out how tomato seeds might grow in space.

germinate sprout
acceleration speeding up
deceleration slowing down

What Is Tomatosphere?

Tomatosphere encourages students from across Canada, the United States, and several other countries to **germinate** tomatoes from seeds. Some of these seeds have been on the International Space Station for as long as 19 months. They've been exposed to weightlessness, intense **acceleration** and **deceleration**, and increased radiation. Scientists want to know how seeds might change as a result of these conditions. Will seeds grow more quickly or more slowly? Will their fruit be as nutritious as fruit grown on Earth?

Why Tomatoes?

Tomatoes are ideal plants for space food. Tomato seeds are light, take up very little space, and sprout quickly. The fruit are very nutritious, preserve well, and can be eaten many ways.

But tomato plants could do a lot more than just provide food for the astronauts to eat. Plants use water, light, and carbon dioxide to make the food they need. This process would use up the carbon dioxide that the astronauts breathe out, preventing it from building up in the spacecraft.

Plants also return oxygen to the air, which would make the air better for the astronauts to breathe. And through evaporation, the leaves of the tomato plants could produce purified water. What a multi-tasking plant!

Will tomatoes grow differently in space? Canadian astronaut Bob Thirsk examines some plants from the Tomatosphere project. With him is Theresa Rondeau-Vuk of the University of Guelph.

Space Farmers

Tomatoes are just one of the many foods that astronauts need in space. Scientists still have a lot to learn about the best ways to grow plants far from Earth. Students taking part in Tomatosphere are helping experts gather the information they need. And who knows—maybe some of those students will one day eat tomatoes in space!

MEDIA WATCH

Look in the media for reports on recent space experiments. What important information did you learn? How do you know if the source is reliable and the information is up-to-date?

DIG DEEPER

1. Use the headings to summarize the most important information about space tomatoes.

2. If you were going to Mars, which vegetable would you like to grow on the journey? Explain your choice to a partner.

A Star Is Born

by Michael George
Illustrated by Jeff Dixon

What are the stages in the life of a star?

Once a star begins to shine, its surface churns with currents, turbulence, and huge waves of gas.

Stars, like people, are born and eventually die. During their lives, stars change in remarkable ways.

From Dust Ball to Star Shine

nebula a cloud of gas and dust that is visible in the sky

A star is born in a giant cloud of gas and dust called a **nebula**. Some nebulae contain small, dense balls of dust and gas called globules. Bit by bit, a globule may grow in size. After millions of years, the globule is a dense, heavy globe, hundreds of times larger than the Earth.

As the globe continues to grow, matter inside it is pressed together more tightly. The increased pressure makes the temperature at the centre of the globe extremely hot. Eventually, the core becomes so hot that the star begins to glow, or shine.

Popcorn!

After about 10 billion years, most stars begin to run out of fuel. With less energy flowing toward the surface, the star begins to shrink. As the core of the star is squeezed, it grows hotter and hotter. The **atoms** in the core begin to "melt" together. This releases more energy and causes the star to burst, a bit like a piece of popcorn.

These enlarged stars are called **red giants**. Red giants are enormous stars. Most are about 60 to 80 million kilometres across, or about 50 times wider than the Sun!

Eventually, the star begins to shrink again, and the temperature of the core rises. Soon it becomes so hot that the star explodes. It hurls its outer layers of gas into space.

When a star explodes, a circle of gases surrounds it.

READ LIKE A WRITER

What words or phrases does the writer use to show the sequence of events?

atom a tiny unit of matter that can exist alone or in combination

red giant a star whose core is melting and expanding

Black Dwarfs and Black Holes

white dwarf a star that has run out of fuel but is still hot enough to shine

black dwarf a star that has lost all its heat and fuel

black hole an area of space with very strong gravity, created when a very large star collapses

The remaining star, now called a **white dwarf**, shines dimly through the cloud of gas and dust. A white dwarf has no source of new energy but continues to glow because it is hot. Given time, the white dwarf loses heat into space and finally turns into a dark globe—a **black dwarf**.

Stars that are 10 or 20 times larger than the Sun end their lives in the most dramatic fashion of all. When a star this big runs out of fuel, its tremendous gravity causes it to collapse. This sets off a violent explosion called a supernova. The supernova hurls the outer layer of the star into space. But the core gets packed more and more tightly, until the star itself is crushed out of existence. All that remains is its intense gravitational field, known as a **black hole**.

The gravity of a black hole is so strong that nothing within a certain distance can resist its pull. A black hole can engulf stars, planets, and entire solar systems. Whatever enters a black hole is lost from this universe forever. Nothing, not even a beam of light, can escape.

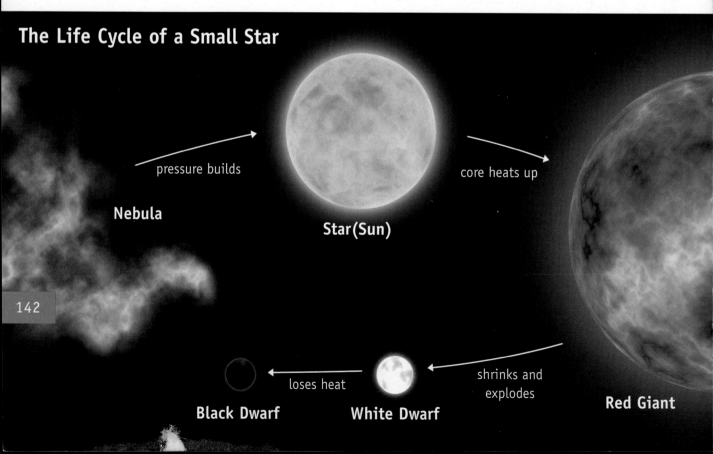

The Life Cycle of a Small Star

Nebula — pressure builds → Star(Sun) — core heats up → Red Giant

Red Giant — shrinks and explodes → White Dwarf — loses heat → Black Dwarf

What do you think of when you look at images of outer space, such as this one of a spiral galaxy?

The Meaning of Stars

During their long lives, stars create the elements that make up the planets, including Earth. The stars also hint at the immensity of our universe and the vastness of time. The next time you stare into the night sky, think about these wonders of space.

DIG DEEPER

1. Make a list of questions that you still have about stars. Beside each question, list one source you could use to find the answer.

2. Create a book aimed at students in a younger grade about the life cycle of a small star. Think about how you can make your explanation clear and interesting for your readers.

Researchers at Work!

Scientists are constantly uncovering new facts about space. You can find out what they have discovered through research.

Choose Your Topic

- Think about space-related topics you have discussed, viewed, and read about.
- With a partner, brainstorm a list of "why" and "how" questions about these topics.
- Select one of your questions for further research.

Plan Your Research

- Find resources you can use to get information about your topic.
- Write down the title, author, and other important information about each resource.
- Decide how you will record the information you find.

RESEARCH TIPS

- Identify keywords to help you search for information.
- Locate information in books, in magazines, and on the Internet.
- Find out when the information was written to make sure it is up-to-date.

Organize Your Information

- Organize your facts around two or three main ideas. Include supporting details for each of these ideas.
- Look for connections among pieces of information.
- Use a chart, outline, or web to arrange your facts logically.

Share Your Research

- Think about who your audience will be.
- Choose an interesting way of presenting the information.
- Consider using features such as diagrams, visuals, and headings to help explain your ideas.

PRESENTATION POINTERS

You could

- present your information as a question-and-answer interview
- build a Web page
- create a bulletin board display
- prepare a multimedia presentation

Canada from Space

How can images from space help us see our planet in new ways?

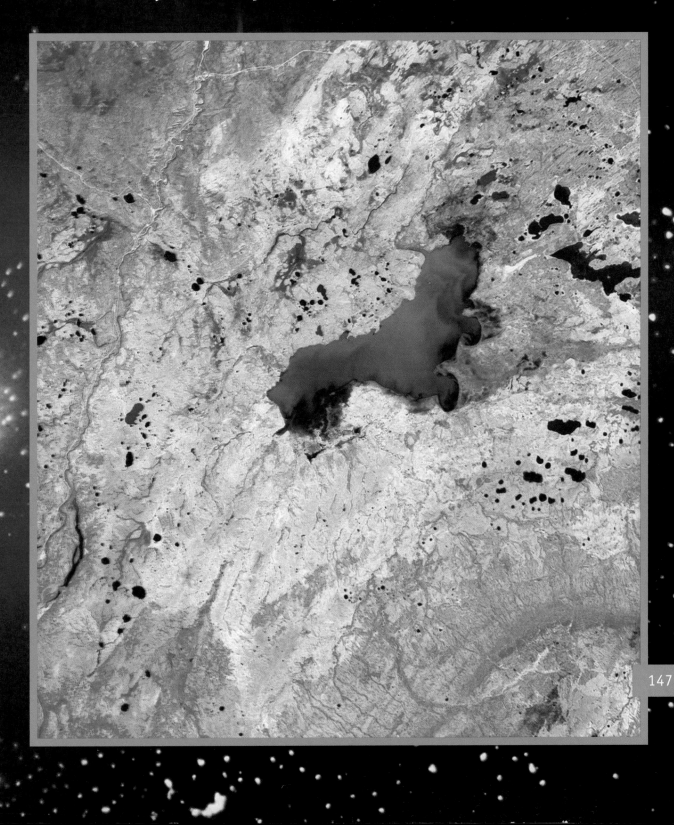

DIG DEEPER ···

1. What physical features can you identify in these images?
2. Work with a partner to think of words or phrases that describe
   these images. Share your two best descriptions with the class.

PLUTO No Longer a Planet!

by Keltie Thomas   Illustrated by Dave Whamond

If Pluto had a personality, what would it be like?

In 2006, astronomers voted to kick Pluto out of the planet club. Now, in an exclusive interview with reporter Ace Astro, the remote ice princess speaks her mind about this shocking decision.

Reporter Ace Astro: Where were you when you heard that you were no longer considered a planet?

Ice Princess Pluto: I was at the outer edge of the solar system, wandering around the Sun accompanied by my moon, Charon.

RAA: How did you feel when the news hit you?

IPP: I laughed! After all, for 75 years astronomers believed I was a planet! Now they suddenly decide I'm just a piece of celestial trash left over from the formation of the solar system. Meanwhile, I haven't changed one iota. I'm the same icy sphere I've been for billions of years.

150

RAA: Did you see it coming?

IPP: Oh, yes. Astronomers had been debating my "planethood" for years. Some said I was too small to be a planet, while others said the shape of my orbit was too odd. I have never really fit in with the other planets, you know. Just call me an oddball!

RAA: What do you say to those who think you haven't got what it takes to be a planet?

IPP: According to astronomers' new definition, planets must orbit the Sun, be round, and dominate their neighbourhood by sweeping up asteroids, comets, and any other small bits and pieces in their path. Well, I zip around the Sun and I'm round, but I certainly don't push other celestial bodies around—I'm no bully! If that's what it takes to be a planet, I say no thank you!

RAA: What do you think the future holds for you?

IPP: I think the future will reveal what I really am. Since I'm so far away from Earth, you can't possibly see me with the naked eye. However, in 2015, a spacecraft called *New Horizons* will visit me from Earth, and I'm confident it will reveal my true nature for the entire world to see.

MEDIA WATCH

Watch for interviews about space topics on the Internet, in newspapers, in magazines, or on television. What is fact and what is opinion? How do you know?

AS PLUTO TURNS

- Pluto is about one-fifth the size of Earth.
- A day on Pluto lasts almost a week on Earth (6.39 days).
- Pluto takes 247.7 Earth years to orbit the Sun once.
- The average temperature on Pluto is a bone-chilling –236°C.

DIG DEEPER

1. How would you describe Pluto's personality in this selection? Try out different voices to capture her character.

2. With a partner, present this selection as a radio or TV interview using the voice you chose. Think of one or two new questions to include in your interview, and write answers that reflect Pluto's personality.

CAUTION
REDUCE
SPEED

28000
km/h

ASTRONAUTS
AT WORK

SPACE STATION
CONSTRUCTION

CAUTION

What is it like to live in space?

READ LIKE A WRITER

What words do the astronauts use to signal that they are making a comparison?

While living in space, astronauts have to do the same things that you have to do on Earth to stay alive and healthy. They have to eat, breathe, sleep, exercise, and stay clean. How do they do these activities in a weightless environment on the faraway International Space Station (ISS)? Some lucky students got a chance to ask our Canadian astronauts about life on the ISS. Here are their questions and the astronauts' responses.

SPEED
LIMIT
28000

Q **What are some of the sensations that you experience in microgravity?**

On Earth, blood is pumped out by the heart. Gravity helps to send it to the extremities of the body, like the legs. In microgravity, blood and other fluids tend to pool above the upper torso, or chest area, and in the sinuses. Our legs become skinnier and our heads expand to make room for all this new fluid. As a result, we often have headaches due to sinus pain and inflammation. We even find it hard to identify the taste of foods.

153

What chores do you do in space?

On Earth, dust falls gently to the ground, so we have to dust, sweep, and vacuum often. In space, since we're weightless, nothing ever falls to the floor! As the dust slowly drifts around in the air, it gets caught in the filters of our fans. To remove the dust from the filters, we use grey tape with the sticky side out. We also have a little vacuum cleaner to get at the filters in hard-to-reach places. Spills float away and stick to the walls of the spacecraft. To clean up, we have to wipe down the walls with wet wipes. But we don't do dishes! Food and beverages come in their own packages, and we throw the empty containers into our dry trash. Finally, we have to clean the toilet every day, to make sure it doesn't overfill, and to keep it hygienic.

Do you exercise while on the Space Station?

Exercising in space is very important, especially on longer space missions, such as our stay on the International Space Station. We must exercise two hours a day while living on the station. We use a stationary bicycle and treadmill to exercise our upper and lower body muscles. A series of straps and restraints holds us securely against the exercise equipment.

Q Is it difficult to eat in space?

Eating in space is certainly different from eating on Earth, mainly because of the absence of gravity. On Earth, food remains on our plates as we eat. Liquids are easily poured into glasses or drunk directly from cartons or bottles. In a microgravity environment, however, there are no forces at work to keep food and beverages from floating. Loose food would float around the spacecraft, making it particularly difficult to eat. Dangerous situations could occur if food particles are caught in the Space Station's systems.

Foods that might generate small particles are kept in containers. Some foods, such as peas and beans, are usually prepared in a sauce so that they stick to our utensils. We also use squeeze bottles and drinking bags with sealable straws to drink fruit juices, coffee, or tea.

Are there beds on the Space Station?

Astronauts who live on the Space Station for long periods of time have sleep stations. These stations are enclosed compartments, stacked one on top of another like bunk beds. Each station has its own sleeping bag, pillow, light, air vent, and place to store personal belongings.

When we are tired, we put our boots and outer clothing into the sleep station's storage area. Then we climb into our sleeping bags and pull up the long zipper, leaving our arms outside the bag. We snap together the straps around our waists to hold us securely in the bunk. Finally, we slip our hands through loop straps by our sides, so our arms won't float up in front of us while we sleep.

We can close the compartment doors of the sleep stations to reduce outside light and have some extra privacy. These sleep bunks are also equipped with a communications station. This allows the mission controllers on Earth to talk to us if a message needs to get through while we are sleeping.

DIG DEEPER

1. Make a chart to compare daily life on Earth with life in space. Arrange the information on your chart in categories, such as eating, sleeping, etc.

2. With a partner, brainstorm a list of at least three questions you would like to ask a Canadian astronaut about life in space. Where could you find the answers?

Coyote Creates the Big Dipper

by C. J. Taylor

How can a traditional tale explain what we see in space?

READ LIKE A WRITER
What words does the
writer use to signal time
changes?

It was Coyote who placed the stars in the night sky. He was very proud of his work. "I am a fine artist," he would brag to anyone who would listen, his nose pointing to the heavens.

One evening, Coyote was taking a leisurely stroll and admiring the sparkling points of light overhead when he noticed an empty black space near the Bear Star. When he got to the top of his favourite mountain, a spot where he could see the whole universe, he sat down for a moment. He turned his head from side to side. "I shall have to think about this," he said. Coyote continued his evening stroll, deep in thought.

Soon he came upon a pack of wolves and their dog. They were sitting on a cliff, their noses pointing skyward. They were discussing the Bear Star. Now, sometimes Coyote is very sneaky. He hid behind a tree to watch and listen.

"It is impossible to hunt a bear so far away," said one of the wolves. "Let us be on our way."

Suddenly Coyote had an idea. As the wolves and their dog turned to leave, he jumped out from his hiding place. "Hello, cousins. I noticed you admiring the Bear Star. He is indeed a fine bear."

"Yes, it is true, cousin." The largest of the wolves stepped forward. "But he is too far away, and there is no trail for us to follow. We will take our hunt elsewhere."

"I can help you," Coyote boasted, sitting down in front of the wolf, his bushy tail curled around his skinny front legs.

"Sometimes, cousin, your assistance is more trouble than it's worth," replied the wolf. Everyone knew how much Coyote liked to play tricks.

"I only wish to help my relatives." Coyote moved aside as the wolves and their dog made their way down the trail. "It is such a fine bear and you are such good hunters. What a shame!" The pack stopped and gazed skyward. It was indeed a fine bear.

"What do you propose, Coyote?" asked the leader. "We want none of your tricks, mind you," he warned, baring his long white fangs.

"Of course not," said Coyote.

They all gathered around to hear Coyote's plan. "As you know, cousins, it was I who placed the stars in the skyworld. So, does it not make sense that I would know the trail?"

The wolves and dog agreed. "All right, we will follow your trail," said the leader, not quite trusting his crafty cousin.

"First I must fetch my travel bundle," said Coyote. He dashed off into the woods. Just as quickly, he returned with a tattered bundle. He unrolled the old hide. Before them lay a bent and badly strung bow and several crooked arrows.

Coyote proudly announced, "This is our trail. These are magic arrows. I will shoot them into the sky and we will climb up to the Bear."

The pack leader showed his teeth. "You take us for fools, Coyote. Such bent and twisted arrows are useless." The other wolves and the dog began to growl and snap their teeth. The hair stood up on their backs.

Sometimes Coyote can think fast. "It is the same trail Bear used. The bow and arrows may seem bent and crooked, but they are shaped to fit my arms."

The wolves and dog gave that some thought. They growled among themselves.

"Well, if you are not interested, no harm done. I will be on my way." Coyote started to bundle up the crooked arrows and the bent bow. As if speaking to himself, he muttered, "It is such a shame. Such a fine bear. A nice fat bear like that would feed a family for a long time."

Holding the bundle he paused to gaze skyward. "Yes, a shame. Oh, well. Good hunting to you, cousins." As he turned to leave, Coyote heard more growling. This time it was their stomachs.

"Hold on, Coyote. We did not mean to doubt you. Being hungry makes us short-tempered. Please show us the trail," said the leader.

"Very well," replied Coyote. "But you must listen to my instructions. We may be in for danger."

Such a fine bear.

A nice FAT bear ...

Once more, he unrolled the tattered bundle. He reached for the bent bow and one of the crooked arrows. He took careful aim. The arrow twisted and turned toward the sky and held fast in a cloud that misted over the mountaintops. One after another the arrows whizzed from Coyote's bow. Each was planted firmly in the clouds until a ladder had formed right up to the Bear Star. In great amazement the wolves and dog shouted, "This time Coyote's magic works!" They climbed the ladder trail skyward.

Coyote led the way. When he reached the last arrow near the Bear Star, he stopped. "This is where you must follow my instructions carefully," he told the leader, the largest of the wolves. "Step into the sky. Dog, you follow, then the rest." All took their places, waiting for further instructions, as Coyote pranced up and down the shaft of the top arrow. "No. No. That's not right." He pointed to each. "You, go over there. You, go there." The wolves and dog ran every which way, becoming more and more confused. By the time Coyote shouted, "That's it. Perfect!" they were worn out.

The leader called out, "Let us sit awhile and watch Bear while we rest." But soon the wolves and the dog fell asleep. Coyote quickly descended the trail, pulling out each arrow as he ran, dropping a few along the way. When he reached the Earth, he returned to his favourite mountaintop where he could see the whole universe. His tail curled around the bent arrows. When he looked up into the night sky at the Bear Star, there sat the wolves and their dog, and there they would hunt Bear forever. Turning his head from side to side Coyote said, "I am a wonderful artist, and clever too!"

You!

Go
over
there!

DIG DEEPER

1. Work in a group to present a role play of this tale. Try to make your characters as convincing as possible.

2. Traditional tales in First Nations cultures may answer a question about why something exists or how something was formed. Write your own tale that explains something about the stars, moon, planets, or another aspect of space.

secrets

by Myra Cohn Livingston

Space keeps its secrets
hidden.

It does not tell.

Are black holes time machines?
Where do lost comets go?

Is Pluto moon or planet?

How many, how vast
unknown galaxies beyond us?

Do other creatures
dwell   on distant spheres?

Will we ever know?

Space is silent.

It seldom answers.

But we ask.

READ LIKE A WRITER

What techniques do the
poets use to create a
sense of wonder?

SATELLITIS

by Robert Priest
Illustrated by Victor Gad

Well I woke up one morning being circled by a stone
which spun around about my head as cold and white as bone
I reached and tried to stop it but it quickly moved away
and kept on spinning cold and white, all the rest of the day

That night I heard a snapping sound
when I bent to tie my shoe
and what had once been one cold stone, now, alas, was two
I tried again to grab them as they slowly circled me
The clock struck ten I looked again
and there, Oh No! were three

I went at once to the doctor
but when I knocked upon her door
I heard another snapping crack and then I counted four
Four cold white stones a-whirling round
I prayed I would survive
The doctor said "Hey how ya doing"
I blinked and there were five

"Nothing to fear" the doctor said—
"Just too many cheese-eating nights
and so you've developed this nasty rash
called circuitous satellites
You'll have to stop eating your limburger cheese
and sleep for 12 afternoons
In pure and simple layman's terms
you've developed a case of the moons
They come as small as these pebbles here
but as large as weather balloons
In any case there's this to face—
you've gotta bad case of the moons."

She cured me with a backward spin, a somersault and slide
confusing the moons so they began one by one to collide
'til one was left and it did a dive, a jump and a pirouette
I spun it off with a twirling cough and she caught it in a net

By the time I left the doctor's place it was late at night
It felt so good to lose at last those pesky satellites
but that was when I looked at the sky and felt the pain of scars
and wept to see the whole wide world
had a terrible case of the stars, the stars
a terrible case of the stars

DIG DEEPER

1. In a small group, decide on a way to perform one of the poems. Then present your performance to the class.

2. Write your own poem about space. It could be serious like "Secrets" or funny like "Satellitis."

CAPTAIN ARSENIO

INVENTIONS AND MISADVENTURES IN FLIGHT

by Pablo Bernasconi

What strange ways of flying could someone dream up?

The End and
the Beginning

Manuel J. Arsenio was a careless cheese master, blacksmith, scuba diver, and ship captain. Though he was given the easiest of missions in each of these careers, he still couldn't complete any of them successfully. This problem may be the reason he left those jobs behind to enter the distinguished pages of aviation history.

One day in 1782, Captain Arsenio decided to build the first in a long series of eccentric projects that would change his life. And although he had little knowledge of physics or mechanics and had access only to useless materials, he demonstrated great patience and determination throughout the course of his flight experiments.

How do we know about Captain Arsenio? His diary was found by chance, under circumstances to be discussed later. In its 90 pages full of doodles, notes, and technical writings, Arsenio developed 18 different designs for a flying machine, each one original, foolish, and fantastic. Here we explore two of the 18 most influential projects that have contributed to modern aviation.

"Why can birds fly and we humans cannot? What cruel destiny stops all people from seeing the world from above, tasting the clouds, and undoing long distances by air?"

— Captain Arsenio, June 7, 1783

FLIGHT DIARY 1: Motocanary

> "Carts are dragged along by horses, sleighs by dogs, and plows by bulls. I think that if I concentrate enough birds together, the sustaining force will help me win the clouds. It cannot fail!"
>
> — Captain Arsenio, February 18, 1784

2 I start running, and the birds accept the challenge. The glory is mine, mine!

1 The selection process is demanding and exhausting. I accept only those who have wings.

3 My feet leave the ground and I have control of the height. My bones feel the change. I'm almost another bird.

| Phase 1: 14 h | Phase 2: 10 min | Phase 3: 4.5 s |

NOTE: As improbable as it appears, this diary shows us that the Motocanary did fly for a short distance before

READ LIKE A WRITER

How does the writer organize information in the Flight Diaries?

6 The Motocanary needs improvement:

a) I must choose more obedient birds.

b) I must test the design in a field, without any trees.

c) I must always carry a ladder with me.

5.84 m

flight without motor

3.7 m

tree landing

4 It seems that, without warning, some of the engines have changed directions. They are not going where I want them to go!

5 The change of direction causes the rope to break. (Note to self: Next time, use iron cables instead of woollen rope.) I'm headed dangerously close to that tree.

1 m

0 m

167

| Phase 4: 2 s | Phase 5: 1 s | Phase 6: total elapsed time—2 days, 14 h, 10 min, 7.5 s |

crashing into a tree. Maybe the failure is due to Captain Arsenio's misplaced trust in the unreliable canaries.

FLIGHT DIARY 2: Flying Runner

> "I can leave the ground by the effort of an energetic run, transferred to the little wings and multiplied 30 times by the transfer pulleys. It cannot fail!"
>
> — Captain Arsenio, March 23, 1785

1 Countdown to zero. I'm preparing for the big run. I've got faith.

2 I start the acceleration, and the wings seem to be in working order. But I'm not elevating yet.

3 The machine starts to rise at maximum speed. I'm starting to get very tired.

4 All systems go, the balance is controlled—the prototype is a success...up until this point.

| Phase 1: at rest | Phase 2: 21 min | Phase 3: 47 s | Phase 4: 1 min |

NOTE: The reader may notice that there are significant differences between what is written and what actually happened. This

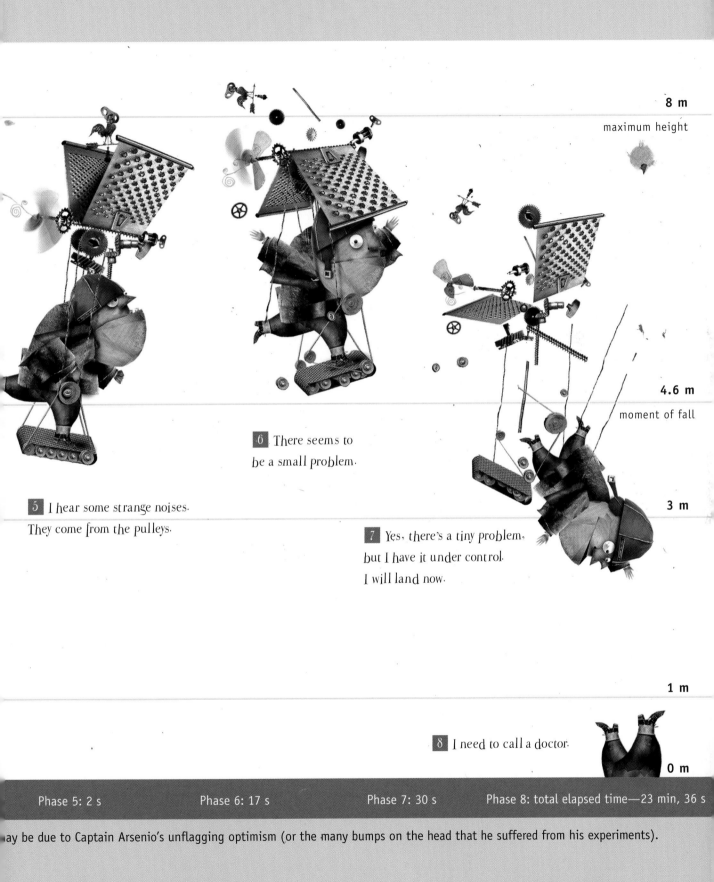

8 m

maximum height

4.6 m

moment of fall

6 There seems to be a small problem.

5 I hear some strange noises. They come from the pulleys.

7 Yes, there's a tiny problem, but I have it under control. I will land now.

3 m

1 m

8 I need to call a doctor.

0 m

Phase 5: 2 s   Phase 6: 17 s   Phase 7: 30 s   Phase 8: total elapsed time—23 min, 36 s

...ay be due to Captain Arsenio's unflagging optimism (or the many bumps on the head that he suffered from his experiments).

Goodbye from Below

As it happens with some legends, multiple versions contradict one another, proof disappears, and word of mouth constructs stories that differ greatly from the reality. No one knows for certain exactly what happened to Captain Arsenio and his flying machines. All that is left is his diary—90 pages of consecutive failures—and one big question: Did he eventually succeed?

Some say that Arsenio's book was buried near Cairo, Egypt—about 12 000 km away from where he lived in Patagonia, Argentina. Others disagree and tell us it was in a chest at the bottom of the sea, buried under a pile of rusty metal junk. But most people insist with determination that Captain Arsenio's diary was found on the surface of the moon on July 20, 1969.

> "Many years have passed since that first Motocanary. Although I have failed many times, I have learned so much. And today, for the first time, I am sure that this new machine I have developed is going to work. I am going for it!"
>
> — Captain Arsenio, December 6, 1789

DIG DEEPER

1. Pretend you are a radio broadcaster assigned to cover one of Captain Arsenio's attempts at flying. With a partner, present for your listeners a play-by-play of what is happening.

2. Create your own amazing flying machine. Make a sketch of your invention, with labels to tell about its wondrous parts.

THE BLUE PLANET

BY ROBERT J. SAWYER

ILLUSTRATED BY PAUL McCUSKER

HOW MIGHT A SCIENCE-FICTION WRITER IMAGINE THE POSSIBILITY OF LIFE ON MARS?

The round door to the office in the underground city opened.

"Teltor! Teltor!"

The director of the space-sciences hive swung her eyestalks to look wearily at Dostan, her excitable assistant. "What is it?"

"Another space probe has been detected coming from the third planet."

"Again?" said Teltor, agitated. She spread her four exoskeletal arms. "But it's only been a hundred days or so since their last probe."

"Exactly. Which means this one must have been launched *before* we dealt with that one."

Teltor's eyestalks drooped as she relaxed. The presence of this new probe didn't mean the people on the blue planet had ignored the message. Still…

"Is this one a lander, or just another orbiter?"

"It has a streamlined component," said Dostan. "Presumably it plans to pass through the atmosphere and come to the surface."

"Where?"

"The South Pole, it looks like."

"And you're sure there's no life on board?"

"I'm sure."

Teltor flexed her triple-fingered hands in resignation. "All right," she said. "Power up the neutralization projector; we'll shut this probe off, too."

• • •

That night, Teltor took her young daughter, Delp, up to the surface. The sky overhead was black—almost as black as the interior of the tunnels leading up from the buried city. Both tiny moons were out, but their wan glow did little to obscure the countless stars.

Teltor held one of her daughter's four hands. No one could come to the surface during the day; the ultraviolet radiation from the sun was deadly. But Teltor was an astronomer—and that was a hard job to do if you always stayed underground.

READ LIKE A WRITER

Why has the writer separated the story into parts?

173

Young Delp's eyestalks swung left and right, trying to take in all the magnificence overhead. But, after a few moments, both stalks turned to the bright blue star near the horizon.

"What's that, Mama?" she asked.

"A lot of people call it the evening star," said Teltor, "but it's really another planet. We're the fourth planet from the Sun, and that one's the third."

"A whole other planet?" said Delp, her mandible clicking in disbelief.

"That's right, dear."

"Are there any people there?"

"Yes, indeed."

"How do you know?"

"They've been sending space probes here for years."

"But they haven't come here in person?"

"No," Teltor said sadly, "they haven't."

"Well, then, why don't we go see them?"

"We can't, dear. The third planet has a surface gravity almost three times as strong as ours. Our exoskeletons would crack open there." Teltor looked at the blue beacon. "No, I'm afraid the only way we'll ever meet is if they come to us."

• • •

"Dr. Goldin! Dr. Goldin!"

The NASA administrator stopped on the way to his car. Another journalist, no doubt. "Yes?" he said guardedly.

"Dr. Goldin, this is the latest in a series of failed missions to Mars. Doesn't that prove that your so-called 'faster, better, cheaper' approach to space exploration isn't working?"

Goldin bristled. "I wouldn't say that."

"But surely if we had human beings on the scene, they could deal with the unexpected, no?"

• • •

Teltor still thought of Delp as her baby, but she was growing up fast; indeed, she'd already shed her carapace twice. Fortunately, though, Delp still shared her mother's fascination with the glories

of the night sky. And so, as often as she could, Teltor would take Delp up to the surface. Delp could name many of the constellations now—the zigzag, the giant scoop, the square—and was good at picking out planets, including the glaringly bright fifth one.

But her favourite, always, was planet three.

"Mom," said Delp—she no longer called her "Mama"—"there's intelligent life here, and there's also intelligent life on our nearest neighbour, the blue planet, right?"

Teltor moved her eyestalks to indicate "yes."

Delp spread her four arms, as if trying to encompass all of the heavens. "Well, if there's life on two planets so close together, doesn't that mean the universe must be teeming with other civilizations?"

Do you know why the third planet is blue ?

Teltor opened her spiracles in gentle laughter. "There's no native life on the third planet."

"But you said they'd been sending probes here."

"Yes, they have. But the life there couldn't have originated on that world."

"Why?"

"Do you know why the third planet is blue?"

"It's mostly covered with liquid water, isn't it?"

"That's right," said Teltor. "And it's probably been that way since shortly after the solar system formed."

"So? Our world used to have water on its surface, too."

"Yes, but the bodies of water here never had any great depth. Studies suggest, though, that the water on the third planet is, and always has been, very deep."

"So?"

Teltor loved her daughter's curiosity. "So, early in our solar system's history, both the blue planet and our world would have been constantly pelted by large meteors and comets—the debris left over from the solar system's formation. And if a meteor hits land or a shallow body of water, heat from the impact might raise temperatures for a short time. But if it hits deep water, the heat would stay longer. It would make the planet too hot to sustain life. A stable environment suitable for the origin of life would have existed here eons before it would have on the third planet. I'm sure life only arose once in this solar system—and that it happened here."

"But—but how would life get from here to the blue planet?"

"That world has strong gravity, remember? Some of the material that was knocked off our world by impacts would eventually get swept up by the blue planet, falling as meteors there. And, of course, many forms of microbes can survive the long periods of freezing that would occur during a voyage through space."

Delp regarded the blue point of light, her eyestalks quavering with wonder. "So, the third planet is really a colony of this world?"

"That's right. All those who live there now are the children of this planet."

• • •

Rosalind Lee was giving her first press conference since being named the new administrator of NASA.

"It's been five years since we lost the Mars Climate Orbiter and the Mars Polar Lander," she said. "And, even more significantly, it's been thirty-five years—over a third of a century!—since Neil Armstrong set foot on the moon. We should follow that giant leap with an even higher jump. For whatever reason, many of the unmanned probes we've sent to Mars have failed. It's time some people went there to find out why."

• • •

The door to Teltor's office opened. "Teltor!"

"Yes, Dostan?"

"Another ship has been detected coming from the blue planet—and it's huge!"

Teltor's eyestalks flexed in surprise. It had been years since the last one. Still, if the inhabitants of planet three had understood the message—had understood that we didn't want them dumping mechanical junk on our world, didn't want them sending robot probes, but rather would only welcome them in person—it would indeed have taken years to prepare for the journey. "Are there signs of life aboard?"

"Yes! Yes, indeed!"

"Track its approach carefully," said Teltor. "I want to be there when it lands."

• • •

The *Bradbury* had touched down beside Olympus Mons during the middle of the Martian day. The seven members of the international crew planted flags in the red sand and explored on foot until the sun set.

The astronauts were about to go to sleep; Earth had set, too, so no messages could be sent to Mission Control until it rose again. But, incredibly, one of the crew spotted something moving out on the planet's surface.

It was—

No. No, it couldn't be. It couldn't.

But it was. A spindly, insect-like figure, perhaps a metre high, coming toward the lander.

A Martian.

The figure stood by one of the *Bradbury*'s articulated metal legs, next to the access ladder. It gestured repeatedly with four segmented arms, seemingly asking for someone to come out.

And, at last, the *Bradbury*'s captain did.

It would be months before the humans learned to understand the Martian language, but everything the exoskeletal being said into the thin air was recorded, of course. "*Gitanda hatabk*" were the first words spoken to the travellers from Earth.

At the time, no human knew what Teltor meant, but nonetheless the words were absolutely appropriate. "Welcome home," the Martian had said.

DIG DEEPER

1. Make a story map showing the settings,
   characters, and events of the story.
2. With a partner, read through Teltor's
   explanation of how life began on Earth.
   Make sure you both understand the
   explanation. Then work together to create
   a series of pictures with captions to
   illustrate the process.

Setting 1	Setting 2
Main characters	Main characters
Events	Events
Events when characters meet	

179

Connect and Share

You've read many amazing facts about space. Now it's your turn to share what you've learned. Create a space trivia quiz.

Prepare the questions

- Think about what you have learned in this unit about space. Go back through the selections and pick out at least five interesting facts or pieces of information.

- For each space fact, write a question for your quiz. Give your contestants three possible answers to choose from (only one of them should be correct).

QUIZ TIPS

- Write questions that do not have a straight "yes" or "no" answer.
- Make sure the three answers you provide for each question seem possible.
- After a contestant has answered, tell all players the correct answer. If possible, provide a bit more information about the topic.

Share your quiz

- Share your Space Trivia Quiz with your family members. Ask them the questions and let them guess the answers.

- Afterward, encourage your family to ask questions and share what they know about space.

Spotlight on Learning

Collect

■ Gather your research notes, writing, and projects from this unit.

Talk and reflect

Work with a partner.

■ Together, read the Learning Goals on page 120.

■ Talk about how well you met these goals.

■ Look through your work for evidence.

Select

■ Choose two pieces of work that show how you achieved the Learning Goals. (The same piece of work can show more than one goal.)

Tell about your choices

■ Tell why you chose each piece and what it shows about your learning.

My choices	I want this in my portfolio because...

Reflect

■ What have you learned about reading, researching, and sharing information about science topics?

■ What new information have you learned about space?

181

Acknowledgements

Permission to reprint copyrighted material is gratefully acknowledged. Every effort has been made to trace ownership of all copyrighted material and to secure permission from copyright holders. In the event of any questions arising as to the use of any material, we will be pleased to make the necessary corrections in future printings.

Student Book

Photographs

Cover, i © NASA/JPL-Caltech/R. Hurt/epa/Corbis; **2–3** Glow Images/Alamy; **8 l** SAY Magazine vol. 5 Issue 7, **c** Library and Archives Canada (http://www.biographi.ca/EN/index.html), **tr** Cover of *Chantal Petitclerc: Wheelchair Athlete*, by Edward O'Connor, published by Pearson Canada, **br** Cover of *The Penguin Book of Canadian Biography for Young Readers Vol. II, 1867–1945*, by Barbara Hehner, published by Puffin Canada; **9** Kevin Peterson/Getty Images; **10–15** (push pins) Jupiterimages; **10** Photo by Jean Boulay, www.jeanboulay.com; **11** AP Photo/Thanassis Stavrakis; **12** Denise Grant/Denise Grant Photography; **13** Denise Grant of Denise Grant Photography; **14** Courtesy of Dan Donaldson; **iv, 15** CP PHOTO/Scott Dunlop; **16 t** Dave Greenwood/Getty Images, **b** © Larry Williams/CORBIS; **17** Ray Boudreau; **18–21** (push pins) Jupiterimages; **v tl, 18** Courtesy of Ryan's Well Foundation (www.ryanswell.ca); **19** Mike Dobel/Alamy; **20** Courtesy of Ryan's Well Foundation (www.ryanswell.ca); **21** Courtesy of Ryan's Well Foundation (www.ryanswell.ca); **22** The Toronto Sun, (frame) Shutterstock; **23** Glenbow Archives NA-3740-29, (photo corners) Shutterstock; **24** Library and Archives Canada; **25** CP PHOTO/Tom Hanson, (photo corners) Shutterstock; **26 bl** Jupiterimages, **tl** CafePress.com (www.cafepress.com), **r** CafePress.com (www.cafepress.com); **27 bl** CafePress.com (www.cafepress.com), **tl** CafePress.com (www.cafepress.com); **v tl, 27 tc** CafePress.com (www.cafepress.com); **v tlc, 27 tr** CafePress.com (www.cafepress.com); **27 br** Concept T-Shirts (http://www.concepttshirts.co.uk); **v cr, 28** Edward Westmacott/Alamy; **29** AP Photo/Christine Nesbitt; **30 tl** © Charles & Josette Lenars/CORBIS, **c** © Owen Franken/CORBIS, **bl** © HOWARD YANES/Reuters/Corbis; **31 t** © Owen Franken/CORBIS, **c** © Owen Franken/CORBIS, **b** © Ed Young/CORBIS; **32 t** Transfair, **b** © Bruno Fert/Corbis; **33 t** Nathalie Dulex, **c** © Owen Franken/CORBIS; **34** Ray Boudreau; **35 t** © Louise Gubb/CORBIS SABA, **b** Larry Bones/Getty Images; **36–37** (background) Ray Pietro/Getty Images; **36 t** © Jim Craigmyle/Corbis, **b** © Andersen Ross/Blend Images/Corbis; **37 bl** © David Lawrence/Alamy, **tc** Ron Levine/Digital Vision/Getty Images, **tr** Ray Pietro/Getty Images; **60** Ablestock/Alamy; **61** © Corbis; **63** Hugh Kretschmer/Stone/Getty Images; **64 t** © Comstock/Jupiterimages, **b** Dorling Kindersley Media Library; **65** Dorling Kindersley Media Library; **66 t** © Courtesy of Twentieth Century Fox/Bureau L.A. Collection/Corbis, **vi t, 66 b** Columbia/Kobal Collection; **67** Ronald Grant Archive; **68** Doug Crouch/Brand X/Corbis; **69** Erik Isakson/Rubberball/Getty Images; **70** Jim Craigmyle/Corbis; **71 t** David Ashley/Corbis, **vi b, 71 b** CP/AP Photo/Ben Margot; **72–73** Philip & Karen Smith/Photographer's Choice RF/Getty Images, **73 b** CP/AP Photo/Ben Margot; **74–75** (background) © AbleStock/Jupiterimages; **74** Noel Hendrickson/Digital Vision/Getty Images; **75 tl** Studio Forza/DAJ/Getty Images, **tr** Gareth Brown/Corbis, **bl** Rebecca Emery/CORBIS, **c** Deborah Jaffe/Photodisc/Getty Images,

br CP/AP Photo/Ben Margot; **76 t** © PhotoObjects/ Jupiterimages, **b** © Royalty-Free/Corbis; **77** Ray Boudreau; **vii t, 78–83** Courtesy of Craig Small; **79, 81** (pencil) © Comstock/Jupiterimages; **79–82** (push pin) © liquidlibrary/Jupiterimages; **80 tl** © Comstock/Jupiterimages; **84–87** Courtesy of KCTS Television; **88** CP/AP Photo/Mel Evans; **89 t** Nice One Productions/Corbis, **b** FirstLight; **vii cl, 90 l** Stuart Westmorland/CORBIS, **r** CP Photo/ Fredericton Daily Gleaner/Stephen MacGillivray; **91** Steve Marcus/Reuters/Corbis; **92 t** CP/Tannis Toohey, **c** Firstlight, **b** © Thinkstock/Jupiterimages; **94** Ray Boudreau; **98–99** Angus Fergusson; **100** Amos Morgan/Photodisc/Getty Images; **107** Allan Feildel; **vii br, 108–116** Used by permission of Vérité Films, (paper clip) © PhotoObjects/Jupiterimages; **118** Olivier Ribardiere/Taxi/Getty Images; **119** Sean Justice/Corbis; **120–121** NASA/JPL-Caltech/STScl; **122–125** (background) © Jupiterimages; **viii tl, 122** William Radcliffe/Science Faction/Getty Images; **viii cl, 123 t** © NASA/Roger Ressmeyer/CORBIS; **123 b** Adastra/Taxi/Getty Images; **124 t** NASA Jet Propulsion Laboratory (NASA-JPL); **viii tr, 124 b** © Dennis Scott/Corbis; **125 t** Jason Reed/ Photodisc Green/Getty Images, **b** StockTrek/ Photodisc Green/GettyImages; **126 bl** Canadian Space Agency, **c** Courtesy YES Mag (www.yesmag.ca), **t** Finley-Holiday Films, **br** Cover from *The Amazing International Space Station* by the Editors of YES Mag used by permission of Kids Can Press; **127** Ray Boudreau; **128** © Gunnar Kullenberg/Jupiterimages; **viii br, 130** NASA; **131** NASA; **viii bl, 132** © Robert Marlen/Corbis; **133** © Mike Dobel/Alamy; **134 t** Brad Wilson/The Image Bank/Getty Images, **b** © Bohemian Nomad Picturemakers/CORBIS; **135** Ray Boudreau; **137** Tomatosphere; **138** Tomatosphere; **139** Tomatosphere; **140** NASA; **141** NASA Jet Propulsion Laboratory (NASA-JPL); **143** NASA Jet Propulsion Laboratory (NASA-JPL); **144** George Doyle/ Stockbyte Silver/Getty Images; **145** © MedioImages/ Corbis; **146–149** (background) © Jupiterimages; **ix tr, 146** Received by the Canada Centre for Remote Sensing. Processed by and provided courtesy of RADARSAT International Inc; **147** Digital Vision/ Getty Images; **148** Landsat image received and analyzed by the Canada Centre for Remote Sensing. Pre-processed by and provided courtesy of RADARSAT International Inc. Air photo and background information courtesy of the British

Columbia Ministry of Forests; **149** NASA Johnson Space Center—Earth Sciences and Image Analysis (NASA-JSC-ES&IA); **150–151** (background) © Jupiterimages; **152–153** NASA (Human Space Flight); **154 tl** Shutterstock, **tr** Courtesy of the Canadian Space Agency, **bl** Shutterstock, **br** NASA; **155 t** © NASA/Roger Ressmeyer/CORBIS, **r** Shutterstock; **156 tl** Shutterstock, **tr** From *The Amazing International Space Station*, by the Editors of YES Mag. Used by permission of Kids Can Press, **bl** From *The Amazing International Space Station*, by the Editors of YES Mag. Used by permission of Kids Can Press, **c** NASA (Human Space Flight); **158–159** Jupiterimages; **161** Jupiterimages; **180** © Will & Deni McIntyre/CORBIS; **181** Photodisc Green/Getty Images

Illustrations

iv t, 4–7 Dave Whamond; **v br** "Secret of the Dance" from *Secret of the Dance* by Andrea Spalding and Alfred Scow (Darlene Gait, illustrator), published by Orca Book Publishers, Victoria, BC, Canada, (2006); **19** Deborah Crowle; **30** Deborah Crowle; **38, 41–42** Anne Villeneuve; **43–44, 46, 52** (border) Susan Todd; **93** Philippe Germain; **vii cr, 96–97** Clive Dobson; **vii bl, 101–106** From *The Other Side* © 2005 by Istvan Banyai. Used with permission of Chronicle Books LLC, San Francisco. Visit ChronicleBooks.com; **ix tl, 129, 136–138** Kevin Cheng; **142** Jeff Dixon; **150–151** Dave Whamond; **162–163** Victor Gad; **ix br, 172, 175, 177, 179** Paul McCusker

Text

18–21 "Making Waves: Ryan Hreljac's Fight for Fresh Water" adapted from "A Boy Who Makes a Difference," by permission of Diana Federman. This article first appeared in the *Christian Science Monitor* (www.csmonitor.com); **22–25** "My Grandpa: A Born Fighter" adapted from "A Born Fighter, Grandpa Was the Last of His Kind," by Sharon Lem, *Toronto Sun*, March 31, 2003, by permission; **28–33** "Square and Fair" adapted from OWL Magazine, "Square and Fair," by Clay McLeod, January/ February 2005 OWL. Used with permission of Bayard Presse Canada Inc.; **38–42** "At Your Age?!" excerpted from *Cootie Shots: Theatrical Inoculations Against Bigotry for Kids, Parents and Teachers,* which is copyright © 2001 by Fringe Benefits. Published by

Shared Reading Posters

Photographs